MANAGING
INFORMATION SECURITY
SECOND EDITION

MANAGING INFORMATION SECURITY

SECOND EDITION

Administrative, Electronic, and Legal Measures to Protect Business Information

James A. Schweitzer

Butterworths

Boston   London   Singapore   Sydney   Toronto   Wellington

To the women in my life,
Millie Jane, Marybeth, Mary Ann, Josette, Donna, and Cynthia, for all the
love and interest you've provided.

Library of Congress Cataloging-in-Publication Data

Schweitzer, James A.
    Managing information security : administrative, electronic, and legal measures to protect business information / James A. Schweitzer.—2nd ed.
      p. cm.
    Bibliography: p.
    Includes index.
    ISBN 0-409-90195-4
    1. Computers—Access control.   2. Electronic data processing—Security measures.   3. Business intelligence—United States.   I. Title.
QA76.9.A25S362   1989
658.4'28—dc20   89-32665
                                     CIP

British Library Cataloguing in Publication Data
Schweitzer, James A.
    Managing information security: administrative, electronic, and legal measures to protect business information.—2nd ed.
    1. Computer systems. Security measures
    I. Title
    005.8

    ISBN 0-409-90195-4

Butterworth Publishers
80 Montvale Avenue
Stoneham, MA 02180

10 9 8 7 6 5 4 3 2 1

Printed in the United States of America

Contents

Preface

In beginning work on this second edition of *Managing Information Security*, I was immediately and keenly aware of the changes in business operations wrought by technology in the intervening seven years. Many positions taken in the first edition (reprinted once) now seem oddly out of date.

Some of the marked changes since 1980 are as follows:

1. Most company security directors and managers are now computer literate and are very aware of the importance and content of what we call "computer security." Further, many security managers routinely use personal computers or networked workstations in completing their daily responsibilities.

2. The focus of security concerns is now on distributed systems and networks of computers rather than on the data center and a few timesharing terminals.

3. Industrial espionage is probably at an all-time high. Information is widely recognized as one of the two most critical business resources (the other being people). Information security exposures are numerous and growing in both gravity and points of vulnerability. The business environment includes varieties of risks considered only in science fiction a few years ago.

In this second edition, I have retained the parts of the first version in which readers have expressed interest; otherwise, I have rewritten the book for the 1990s business environment. Most notably, the broad subject of information security is covered in more depth to include protection measures for all three forms—mental, written, and electronic—in light of the fast-moving business environment of the Information Age.

PART I

Information Is Today's Most Valuable Resource

ONE

Information Is the Critical Difference

In September 1987, the American Arbitration Association (AAA) announced an order and opinion in an arbitration of a dispute between IBM Corporation and Fujitsu Limited concerning Fujitsu's use of IBM software in producing IBM-compatible mainframe computer operating systems.[1] The matter of contention between IBM and Fujitsu had been the subject of various suits and agreements since 1983. The AAA's order provided for a complex resolution of the dispute, including

- Continued access to the information of each party by the other, in secured facilities and following precise rules
- The monitoring of compliance with the rules by a technically expert independent supervisor
- An immunity from challenge of information obtained within the order
- A limited time for the life of the order

The extent, cost, and complexity of the arbitration demonstrate the value of the matter in dispute, namely, information on software constructions. In business today, information has become a valuable and necessary resource.

Although an excellent manager with poor information may be able to make some good decisions through intuition, an average manager with quality information will make better decisions consistently. The dynamic business environment today, with intense competition and a very short technology development cycle, means that the company without quality information will suffer a serious competitive disadvantage.

The availability of information plays a key role in reducing risk and uncertainty in decision making. This idea developed during the 1970s into the concept of information resource management (IRM). The basic premise is that information should be treated as a resource of strategic value to organizations.[2,3]

3

CASES

Some examples, derived from actual cases, illustrate the importance of quality information.

Lack of Conclusive Data

Company A was developing a new machine but did not have conclusive data on the reliability of a key component. In the rush to beat a competitor (known to be working on a similar product) to the marketplace, company A decided to go into production. After hundreds of machines had been shipped to customers, a serious, dangerous fault was discovered in the untested component. The product was recalled, and company A lost its market niche. Information lacking integrity was relied on; the result was a business-threatening loss.

Failure to Protect Valuable Information

Company B had been working on a new product with unusual features for a number of years. The product was announced, but shortly thereafter a competitor announced a similar product at lower cost. Company B's management was certain that the competitor had somehow obtained the technical information developed for the new product. Without the cost of development to amortize, the competitive product could be priced much lower. Company B had failed to protect valuable information and thus lost its profit from what should have been a unique product.

Poor-Quality Information

Company C purchased an analysis of the market for an innovative service. Market data indicated that the service would not sell, and plans were canceled. Shortly thereafter a competitor announced a very similar service, which took the market by storm and created a sensation. Company C's definition of the service had been flawed. Poor-quality information led to a decision that eliminated a highly profitable opportunity from company C's plans.

Failure to Protect Research Information

Company D's laboratories had been working on a highly technical and innovative communications product. Certain employees of the company left and founded their own new business. Company D, on discovering that the new company planned to announce a product based on the results of company D's research, sued in court to stop it. The court threw out the case because company D had failed to establish effective programs to identify and protect research results. Company D had failed to recognize the value of research information.

Misunderstood and Misapplied Data

Company E used financial reports prepared on microcomputers by various analysts, using data extracted from central computer databases. An audit revealed that the company had improperly stated business results figures because certain analysts had used microcomputer programs that contained serious flaws; data were thus misunderstood and misapplied. Company E was fined by the Securities and Exchange Commission (SEC).

Unreliable Information Sources

Company F was unable to generate current financial operating data for six weeks because of computer problems. The company lost control of current liquidity and was forced into bankruptcy. Unreliable information sources caused a business to fail.

Computer Hackers

Company G operated a service using a network of computers. Certain computer hackers got into the network and gained control of the company's computer. Eventually, the hackers gained sufficient control to cause the company to shut down the business. The information files were essential to continuing operation, and their threatened destruction put the company and its customers in an untenable situation.

GOOD MANAGEMENT REQUIRES QUALITY INFORMATION

The cases described above show that quality information is essential to businesses today. But what is quality information? It can be defined as *information that meets management requirements for integrity, reliability, and privacy*. These characteristics are provided through proper management and control of information resources. Specifically, quality information results when

- Information is properly identified, classified, and managed as an important resource.

- Information systems and manual information procedures are carefully designed, installed, maintained, and audited.
- Employees are suitably trained and supervised.
- Proper controls and separation of duties are established as appropriate to information value.
- Information security is provided based on established policy covering classification and handling.

Ensuring that quality information is provided for business operation is not a one-shot or cursory effort. Rather, it is a result of carefully planned management efforts that involve almost all aspects of business operations. Part III will examine the management structure and process for achieving quality information.

Characteristics of Quality Information

We have just noted that quality information has characteristics of integrity, reliability, and privacy. We need a clear understanding of these characteristics before we can develop concepts of information value.

Integrity

Integrity means that the information is correct or accurate to the degree anticipated by the people who will use it. For example, accounting data are generally expected to be close to 100% accurate. Although we realize that accounting data do not perfectly describe the real world (the unit manufacturing cost of an item may be accurate only within 10% or so), we expect that summations or analyses of data will be completely free of errors. An accounting report that is missing data or has mathematical errors does not have integrity, even if the errors are fairly small.

A report on a survey of customer satisfaction, however, is expected to be only generally correct. We know that such questions as "how do you like" or "are you satisfied with" necessarily evoke replies that are shaded with various meanings. It is impossible to reply to qualitative survey questions with precise mathematical answers. Therefore, when we read that "90% of our customers are satisfied," we interpret that reply in general rather than in exact terms. A report that provides a good, but not necessarily precise, analysis of customer satisfaction has integrity because it gives us what we expect. A report that summarizes other reports would lack integrity if it did not include one or more of the sources expected, even if it were mathematically precise.

Information sometimes is obviously not precise (e.g., population census data) but at other times users demand and require precision (e.g., designs for computer circuit logic). Information in either case has integrity when it meets users' expectations for correctness and completeness.

Reliability

Reliability means that information is available when and where it is needed. Good management decisions require information that is both correct and current. In large organizations, management also needs information at the proper place.

Thirty years ago, managers controlled a business by considering historical data; at best, reports summarized the previous week or, more probably, the previous month. Today, modern concepts such as "just in time" inventory control demand information on operations almost minute by minute. When information is made available to the people who need it, at the time required, it is reliable.

Computing and telecommunications technologies have provided for spectacular advances in capabilities to develop and deliver information. Reports on critical business activities can be prepared and delivered across the world in minutes. Of course, our expectations about such services have grown along with our abilities. The multinational, worldwide corporation would not be possible without fast communication. Managers have come to demand real-time reporting. Reliable information systems are commonplace; unfortunately, there are exceptions, and managers occasionally lose control because good information is missing.

Information can be lost or delayed because of intentional or unintentional acts by employees or outsiders, especially when extensive networks are in use. Security is an essential consideration when systems are designed and implemented. Proper controls check for information completeness and delivery and prevent penetration, unauthorized changes, and improper diversion of data.

Information then is reliable when the information systems and processes in place can deliver data when and where expected.

Privacy

Privacy refers to protection of information from any unauthorized observation, modification, or diversion. Information may be said to have privacy if it is effectively limited to those persons, computer programs, and manual processes authorized by management. One immediately thinks about personnel records, and properly so, but many other kinds of proprietary information (e.g., research developments, engineering drawings, business strategy reports) must also be ensured privacy.

Security measures are key to ensuring information privacy. The business should have established an information protection policy and have implemented good information-handling practices. As discussed in Chapter 6, there are important legal reasons to have such a program.

Strategic Advantages of Quality Information

Smart managers make use of information to gain advantage over competitors. Astute managers will ensure first that the information they rely on for decision making is quality information. The information used may be internally generated or developed from external sources. Almost every kind of business information can be used to competitive advantage, as can the information processing infrastructure (see Chap. 3). Some information uses are *serendipitous* (unplanned new uses are found for information or information systems already in place) or *synergistic* (ongoing business activity is combined with information resources in some advantageous manner). In other words, businesses often find hidden opportunities when they use existing information resources in imaginative new ways.

The Hoover Commission Report of 1955 suggested that "intelligence deals with all the things which should be known in advance of initiating a course of action." Most managers are directly aware of a body of internally available information used in managing. They are also indirectly aware that other information is collected and used but is perhaps not delivered to them for decision purposes or is not collected in useful forms.

There is also information available outside the company, which can be collected openly or in secret (not necessarily illegally). We can say that the body of information available for management purposes falls into three categories:

1. Strategic information provided internally, including information on research and development, engineering, product design, customer surveys, market analyses, profitability projections, human resources planning, and return on assets
2. Strategic information from outside the company, including market studies, competitors' activities and plans, product opportunities, skills availability studies, and technology developments
3. Operating information provided internally, such as accounting, production, and inventory reports, human resources inventories, cost of manufacturing and of sales, burden costs, administrative overhead costs, customer lists, and records of product placement

Intelligence is the product of the evaluation, analysis, integration, and interpretation of all available information that may affect the company's survival and success.[4] If management takes information seriously, a senior manager should be given responsibility to see that all information that could bear on company strategy is developed, collected, analyzed, and presented in useful form to key decision makers. Very often significant information is collected in the course of business but is overlooked through ignorance of its existence or through carelessness. In other cases, information that could be useful is ignored until it is outdated.

Some examples illustrate the value of information already at hand:

Customer Lists

Company H sold books to libraries, bookstores, and schools. It occurred to one of the managers that company H's customer lists represented a market for various sundry items related to books, such as stationery and school supplies. The company developed a program for accepting orders for supplies through the on-line computer systems used to sell books.

Reference Service

Company J manufactured heavy industrial equipment. To help customers install this equipment, company J maintained a list of recommended riggers and installers. The company realized that businesses that did not buy machinery might also be looking for heavy moving and installation services. A reference service was started, which led to a consulting business, all as a result of considering information already developed.

Employee Teams

Company K, an insurance business, wanted to reduce the administrative costs of writing policies. The company formed teams of employees to develop more efficient methods. Many new and improved processes were suggested and put into use. Several of the ideas had been used for years in smaller groups but had not been communicated to the company at large.

Marketing Department

Company L's senior management asked for a program to develop information about competitors. After a few false starts, it was discovered that the marketing department already had the data needed, which was included in a market survey purchased regularly.

INFORMATION VALUE CYCLES

Computing and telecommunications have increased the amount of information generated and distributed by several orders of magnitude. The same systems have increased the rate of business activities until we now see a very short information cycle. This means that a new concept is developed, implemented, and marketed, and a few months later, another product arrives with yet a better feature. Or, we see actions in the financial markets that must be completed within a brief time to be effective, such as corporate takeovers.

Exposure of such information could mean the loss of a market advantage or a significant cost break for a competitor. For many companies, the investment for a new product is so great that the very life of the business depends on a successful, noncompetitive market introduction (at least for a time).

Certain information may then have extremely high value for a very brief period. A business advantage or profit can be lost if certain data become known to unauthorized parties or if a certain period passes before advantage can be taken of unique information. For the manager concerned about protecting valuable information, this short life cycle means that the traditional procedural methods for protecting information may not be appropriate. Merely arranging for certain people to keep a secret or for certain documents to be stamped "confidential" reflects an unrealistic appraisal of information availability today. In such a circumstance, every employee involved in the product life cycle must be sufficiently aware, knowledgeable, and motivated to ensure that such information is protected at all times. This understanding can be developed only with effort over time. Eastman Kodak Company is one that has a reputation for tight-lipped employees. Kodak has made the confidentiality of its product information an employee creed.

Ensuring that employees regard the company's information as a valuable item to be protected requires a firm policy statement and an on-going program of education and training. Recently, we were told about two employees at company M who were destroying documents from "burn boxes" (boxes in which confidential documents are placed to prevent them from going into the public trash system). The two employees were apparently reading each document before they threw it into the shredder. They apparently had not been given an appreciation of their job, which was to prevent casual perusal by anyone unauthorized, including themselves.

A MANAGEMENT VIEW

Although business writers have been talking about information management for a number of years, very few companies have really done anything about it. In view of the investment of most companies in information (IBM reportedly spends 7% of sales on information systems), it seems strange that most businesses have a chief executive officer (CEO) and a chief financial officer (CFO) but not a chief information officer (CIO). Although some information systems executives may have the title of "information manager," the majority of information executives today spend their time trying to control data processing costs. That is a laudable objective, but the real task for the information executive is to provide information to senior management that will enable the business to become more efficient.

Synnott and Gruber describe the three-step process used by American Can Company (now Primerica) to improve information generation and use.[5] The process included three basic steps:

1. Revising the organization to centralize direction of information management and to ensure that all information activities provide data on productivity and profitability consistently

2. Improving communications between line managers and information providers by putting people with business experience in critical information systems jobs
3. Setting up management information advisory committees in key business areas to establish information priorities, approve systems plans, and monitor information programs

Such an approach begins to deal with the many questions concerning use of information resources. These include the following:

1. What is the basic information element set for this business?
2. How should the business information base be organized to get the most advantageous information to decision makers?
3. What management tasks relate to developing, maintaining, and delivering quality information?

Information is a resource that offers great opportunity to the business that manages, develops, and applies it to making better decisions. But there can be no optimum use of the business information resource unless management addresses the matter with bold decisions. *The Information Edge,* by N. Dean Meyer and Mary E. Boone, describes the application of information to strategic advantage in numerous instances and is recommended for the reader who wishes more information on this aspect of the subject.[6]

TWO

Information Vulnerability: The Threat to Business

The loss or exposure of critical information is a real and increasing threat to business. Information vulnerability can be considered from four viewpoints:

1. *Circumstance* of loss or exposure
2. *Identity* of persons stealing, destroying, or observing the information
3. The *medium* (mental, written, or electronic information forms) involved in the loss or exposure
4. The *value* of the information

INFORMATION RISK CATEGORIES

Circumstance refers to the situation surrounding the loss or exposure (L/E) of information. Some possible circumstances include

- Intentional L/E caused by insiders, usually in the course of business operations
- Unintentional L/E caused by insiders, usually in the course of business operations
- Intentional L/E caused by outsiders, usually external to the normal routine of business operations (e.g., industrial espionage)
- Unintentional L/E caused by outsiders, usually in the course of business operations and involving a consultant or contractor

Naturally, information L/E cases may involve a combination of these circumstances, such as when an employee feeds information to an industrial espionage agent working for a competitor.

The *identity* of the persons involved in information L/E may include

- Trusted employees (those granted access to the information)
- Untrusted employees (those not allowed access to the information)
- Trusted outsiders (e.g., a consultant or contractor)
- Untrusted outsiders

Very often, business managers do not take the trouble to identify which employees should be trusted with highly sensitive information. Rather, they assume general trustworthiness, a line of reasoning not often supported by facts.

The information *medium* involved in information L/E includes

- Mental information, or that information known and remembered by individuals
- Written information, or that information in printed or handwritten form, usually on paper or microforms
- Electronic information, or that information in computers, on tapes or disks, or in transmission over telecommunications networks (data and voice)

The *value* of the information refers to

1.　Objective value, or the importance of the information to the business for continuity or legal purposes. For example, certain financial records may be required by law, or certain records or logs, such as the minutes of the board of directors, may be needed for historical proof. Information with objective value needs protection over extended periods.

2.　Subjective value, or the worth of information that follows from its nature. Customer lists, strategic plans, employee data, and sales records all may have subjective value. Since this kind of information may have a defined life cycle, information with subjective value tends to need protection for only a brief time.

QUANTIFYING INFORMATION VALUES

Usually, we will wish to identify an information element further by some quantitative value expression, such as high, medium, or low value. High-value information, either subjective or objective, should be rigorously protected; high-value data in electronic form should be encrypted, and printed high-value information should be kept in a safe. We may decide that protection of low-value information is not worth the cost.

These information vulnerability viewpoints or categories are important for management consideration because they help us to understand the risks to business information as well as guide us in selecting proper information control and protection measures. As we shall see later, it is possible and practical to protect business information in all three forms (see the Appendixes). Here, we will review today's information vulnerabilities to complete our rationale for information resource management.

ATTACKS ON INFORMATION

We have noted that computer and communications technologies have propelled us into the Information Age. These advances have also made business susceptible to new and dangerous kinds of invisible attacks, popularly generalized as "computer crime." Computer crime is a popular topic for the press and is probably a real threat to businesses. But as of 1989, the most significant threats to critical business information continue to come from the traditional sources, that is, from trusted insiders who are careless with information in mental or written form. This vulnerability includes common errors, probably the most costly information problem. A secondary risk is from trusted insiders who purposely expose or destroy information.

The answer to these kinds of threats is simple and obvious: better training, supervision, and motivation for employees and better systems and procedures to prevent errors and safeguard valuable information. Unfortunately, the regularity and frequency of cases involving exposure or loss of sensitive information show that in many companies, management has not bothered to address the matter effectively.

Risks to business information other than carelessness with paper and loose talk are far less frequent and have less impact. But the potential for information exposure or loss through misuse or penetration of computer or communications systems must be taken seriously. No doubt a time will come when we will regularly learn of significant electronic (or "logical") attacks on business information through connections from in-house or external computers. So far, we are seeing only nuisance attacks (with a few exceptions such as "hacker" attacks by way of software "worms"), but as individual computer user capabilities for connection and penetration increase, we will probably hear about major lawsuits and even business failures resulting from logical information exposures and thefts.

Many people regard industrial espionage as a joke; they cannot imagine that a competitor would actually hire someone to work for a target company in hopes of stealing information. Sadly, this is a serious matter. There *are* industrial spies, and they *do* collect information, some of it legally, some of it under questionable circumstances, and some of it in an outright unethical manner. Information on ethical methods for collecting competitive information can be obtained from materials and training courses offered by Washington Researchers, Washington, D.C., and Information USA, Chevy Chase, Maryland. If a company is careless with its data, even ethical operators will find it no problem to get competitive, proprietary information.

CASES

The cases described below are true. They illustrate circumstance, identity, medium, and value in information L/E. In some instances the names of the companies have been changed, but all these cases were reported, at least locally, when they occurred.

Case 1

During labor contract negotiations, management of a brewery in the United Kingdom was surprised when union negotiators knew details of the company's financial situation and business plans. This knowledge gave the union the ability to predict management's positions on several important issues. Eventually, the brewery traced the information leak to a data center employee who had been taking printed reports home. The employee had found a customer for the information—the union—and had been making additional income by delivering copies of certain business reports.

Analysis:

Circumstance—purposeful exposure by an insider

Identity—trusted insider

Medium—printed report

Value—high subjective value

Did the brewery have an active program to identify valuable information and to train employees how to handle and protect it? Were supervisors aware that information processed was private to the company? Did anyone check what employees leaving the building were carrying?

Case 2

OEC office equipment company was informed by a supplier that a person operating a telephone office supplies marketing operation in southern California was offering OEC customer lists. The price was $10,000 for a list showing customer name and address, equipment at the location, and coded buying history. The lists were being used by a number of small businesses in the area for leads for sales calls. OEC had had a number of complaints from its salespeople about customers being sold cheap merchandise based on false claims of relationship with OEC. Customer lists were regularly provided to OEC salespeople for the particular area covered. These lists, or copies of them, were being offered for sale.

Analysis:

Circumstance—careless or intentional exposure by insiders

Identity—trusted insiders exposing information

Medium—printed listings

Value—medium subjective value

Did the company have a procedure for recovering old lists from salespeople when new ones were issued? Were salespeople aware of the value of such lists? Were lists marked to indicate that they were restricted to OEC only?

Case 3

Several research employees at Texas Instruments (TI) left the company to work in the same technical area at another company. TI discovered that the product being developed there was the same as a new development at TI. In court, various TI people testified that they had not been told that the information concerning the new product was proprietary.

Analysis:

Circumstance—insiders purposely transferring information to a competitor

Identity—trusted insiders (when they gained the data)

Medium—mental, printed, and electronic forms

Value—high subjective value

Did the company have an active information protection program in the research area? Were senior managers driving the program? Were the information media commonly marked with TI value indicators or restrictive warnings?

Case 4

An employee of a major corporation, who had been discharged, was assisted by his supervisor in loading boxes of engineering data into his car. Later, the man attempted to extort money from the corporation by offering to sell back the information.

Analysis:

Circumstance—outsider assisted by insider takes proprietary information

Identity—trusted insider and untrusted outsider

Medium—printed material

Value—medium subjective value

Were the people involved aware of company rules regarding information protection? Had management made clear that the removal of these data would be regarded as a serious matter?

Case 5

An engineering employee of a well-known computer manufacturer was able to use his network connections to put together a detailed description of the technology decisions that formed the basis for a new product. He then sent this description to a number of people, and a portion of the material was published in a technical journal, exposing a sensitive strategic thrust by the company.

Analysis:

Circumstance—insider passed information to outsider

Identity—trusted insider

Medium—information in electronic (digital) form

Value—high subjective value

Did the network have sufficient security for the information files accessed to assemble the description? Was the originator of the description aware of the sensitivity of the data? Had management made clear that such distribution of strategic technical data was a serious breach of regulations?

Case 6

A clerk taking telephone orders for ABC wholesale distributors discovered that orders could be placed for a false delivery address, without her being identified as the originator, by passing information on customer credit to an accomplice. She arranged for her boyfriend to rent a truck and pick up orders set up on the warehouse dock. Over several months, thousands of dollars worth of merchandise were stolen.

Analysis:

Circumstance—insider passing data to outsider

Identity—trusted insider and untrusted outsider

Medium—mental information (by telephone)

Value—medium subjective value

Were customer credit records properly controlled? When clerks accessed various records, were records made and access justified?

In these cases we see that information loss or exposure resulted from two common failings:

1. Management had not identified or had not provided suitable protection for valuable information.
2. Employees were not properly trained or motivated and perhaps believed management really did not take the matter seriously.

INFORMATION VULNERABILITY BY TYPE

Information vulnerability can be categorized as follows:

- *Exposure,* or observation by unauthorized persons (or programs, in the case of electronic information)
- *Destruction* due to accidental or purposeful actions or natural disasters
- *Denial of access* through interference with or destruction of a part of the information processing infrastructure, e.g., a network or computer system
- *Theft,* or the unauthorized removal of information from its proper place of use or storage
- *Unauthorized change,* so as to destroy the integrity of the information

Exposure

Exposure or unauthorized observation of sensitive information usually occurs because individuals are curious or perceive an opportunity to learn certain things. Exposure usually occurs in secret; that is, the persons observing the information do not remove it or destroy it and do not wish the information owner to know that they have it. Industrial espionage is typically a stealthy process of obtaining information. If such observation becomes known, the value of the information to the secret observer may be lessened, since the owner may take secret actions to cancel or reduce the information's value.

When information is in electronic form, unauthorized observation may be easier to do in secret because no physical entry to an office or building may be required. This is especially true when no effective security barriers are placed between an outside caller (e.g., from a home computer) and a database. This has been the case in a number of reported "computer hacker" penetrations.

Although not commonly exposed or discussed in the press, industrial espionage agents do operate in the United States and probably in every industrialized nation. Bottom and Gallati explain that

Employers of espionage agents directed against corporations include hostile nations, competitors, terrorists, and organized crime. Often it is difficult, if not impossible, to discover the real employer of an espionage agent. . . . The corporate information that spies seek appears in a number of forms, including computer-stored data, blueprints, letters or memoranda, files, formulas, charts and diagrams, production models, and prototypes . . . visual observations, and the interception of verbal communications.[7]

With regard to visual observations, it is worthwhile to remember a case involving DuPont, where a competitor used an aircraft to take photographs of a new plant and equipment being installed. There was no roof on the plant because the heavy machinery had to be lowered into place with cranes.

Many times curiosity leads to more serious exposure or loss of information. Employees who are authorized to use a computer system to perform task A may find, to their surprise, that they can also do tasks B and C and can look at records outside their normal purview. Often such a discovery results not only in information exposure but in a perceived opportunity to profit from fraudulent acts (illustrated by the case of the wholesaler on page 18) or even threatened blackmail (e.g., should personnel records be involved). In one case in New York, an employee working on a home computer terminal allowed his teenage son to observe a sign-on procedure. The son took the process to his high school computer class. The students were able to display a list of names identified by the employer for layoff.

Although many times management fails to inculcate employees about the value of information, we often see cases where employees are encouraged by outsiders to recognize opportunities—using the employer's information—for themselves. A data processing supervisor, in France, received a year's wages for spiriting away certain printouts from the company data center.

There are also many instances where valuable information can be exposed merely by having an astute observer with a sharp memory see the data briefly. The best example of a memory transfer of information is the story of how the knitting machine—a key component of the Industrial Revolution—was brought secretly from England to the United States in the memory of one man. Smart executives do not assume that the office cleaners cannot take advantage of information allowed to lie unattended on desks. In an unusual case, an executive from a multinational company entered a telephone booth in a major airport and discovered there a copy of his company's strategic plan for the next year. How many other copies of such documents are left lying in various public places—airplane seats, waiting rooms, clubs—can only be imagined.

An employee of a major research center opened the morning's mail and discovered that a batch of sensitive documents, from a competitor, had been stuffed into an envelope from another company location, probably by the post office. The documents were immediately returned to their owner. Almost all large companies operate according to a high standard of ethical behavior. When a competitor's documents are found or are offered, generally an immediate call is made to the security director of the company owning the data. Because this is not true for every business or every employee, we must continue to worry about industrial espionage.

The most common source of unauthorized observation remains the careless spoken word. No one knows how many business deals were spoiled or promising new product plans derailed by careless talk, but many such cases exist. People like to impress others with their knowledge of "insider" information. Casual conversations in bars and hotel dining rooms often give the skilled listener enough information to piece together a competitive decision. The information may still be complete and valid, but once key elements are exposed, it may shortly be worthless. A senior executive once confided that "we have no rules but we all know how to handle information." If more than two people are included in the "we," it is highly unlikely that the group has a common understanding of what is expected and what information is really valuable.

Destruction

The destruction of information is usually an act of revenge by a disgruntled employee, since it is easier to steal information in most cases. Information can also be destroyed by carelessness in preparation, handling, or processing or by accident, such as a fire or flood. A number of cases of intentional information destruction have been reported in the newspapers. These have usually been incidents involving computer hackers, who erase files in businesses or institutions, probably to demonstrate their knowledge and power. Known political groups, such as the peace movement, have on occasion destroyed various government records.

Any destruction of information is harmful, but businesses generally should be more concerned with observation or theft of information. A disgruntled employee is a risk but is more likely to modify information than to destroy it.

Denial of Access

Information may be whole and safe, but if managers cannot get to it, it is of little value. In most businesses today, critical information is in electronic form for a good part of its useful life. Any interruption in computing or communications services can therefore seriously affect business operations. This is not to say, however, that written or mental information cannot become unavailable.

Business contingency planning is necessary to allow for the chance, however remote, that critical resources may not be available at some point. These critical resources include plant, equipment, raw materials, and information.

Denial of service can be caused by several events, among which are

- Natural disasters
- Fire (by far the most frequent cause in the United States)
- Intentional acts of sabotage by employees or outsiders

Risks of denial of availability for written information are generally in the area of natural disasters or fire. Such events may make the company's offices off limits for an extended time; files may be safe, but people cannot get to them. An accident at a nearby nuclear power plant comes to mind as the ultimate denial of service for written information.

Denial of access to mental information could be caused by a strike of skilled technicians. This is an unusual situation. Perhaps more of a worry is the denial of information that occurs when a key scientist or technical expert resigns to work for a competitor. Good employment and proprietary information contracts are needed for such cases and should be standard practice in every business (see the Appendixes).

Services by computers and access to electronic information bases can be compromised or denied by destruction or disablement of data centers or communications centers, be it accidental or intentional. An accidental tripping of a fire alarm could flood a data center. A fire in another part of a building housing a data center could result in flooding when the fire is put out. Purposeful destruction or disablement of data processing facilities has resulted from bombings or smoke generation, usually for political demonstration purposes. A data center or communications system could also be disabled remotely if a skilled technician is able to penetrate to the operating system and make changes therein or is able to introduce code such as a "worm" or "virus." A computer operator could sabotage a system by cutting wires or pouring soft drinks into the processor.

These are unusual cases; the major risk seems to be from a disaster caused by an accident or by system malfunction. Disaster recovery planning is the usual protection.

Theft

Theft of information has become commonplace, but seldom are there cases where information is completely removed so that the owner is left with nothing. Rather, most cases involve the copying or observing of information, with the original data left in place. This is discussed in the section on unauthorized observation or exposure. In this day of copiers and electronic information files, it is seldom that a purloined document or electronic file cannot be replaced with another from company files or computer backup. Nevertheless, it might be said that unauthorized observation is actually theft of information, since "if I know it, I have it, and it does not belong to me." But we will stick to our strict definition for simplicity.

Once information has been taken and given to a competitor, it may lose its value for the original owner. Many cases involve people in research and product development, the areas in which most information of strategic competitive value is found.

In a number of cases, disgruntled employees have left a company and taken along various technical documents. They then have attempted to sell these documents to competitors, but very often the competitor immediately reported the attempt to the owner of the information and the would-be sellers of information were arrested.

Other cases are not so simple. In one recent investigation, a witness reported seeing a highly classified document in the foreign offices of a competing firm. The owner of the information was never able to prove the case, but the witness's credibility was not questioned and the company was very concerned, more about the channel used to transfer the document than about the information itself.

Industrial espionage is a fact. The famous IBM-Hitachi case, where Japanese agents bought copies of secret IBM documents for Hitachi, is proof. It is interesting to note that the information was all in printed form, although both companies are noted for their use of computers. One wonders why the data were not exchanged as floppy disks; probably because the buyers wanted to examine the merchandise before paying!

Industrial spies may be planted in a company long before they actually steal any information, or current employees may be recruited by friends or relatives. When the owner of information is a large company and the business needing the data is very small, it is easy for people to rationalize a theft of information: It is so important to the little company, and the big one "will never miss it."

Some of these cases have tragic endings. In his book *Trade Secrets*, James Pooley tells about two companies that became enmeshed in lawsuits over ownership of information, resulting in the failure of both.[8]

Finally, one particular kind of data theft is worth noting. Lists of employees, especially executives, are very valuable for marketing purposes of all kinds. Many people tell about being called at work by stockbrokers, probably because someone gave them a company listing. Any kind of personnel list should be marked as company private information and protected accordingly.

Unauthorized Change or Modification

When all business information was in written or mental forms, the written form was the official record, and modification posed some difficulty. One had to get the document and somehow invisibly make changes. It could be done, but it required skill, stealth, and entry to building and office.

Now information can be in electronic form, which is sometimes the only form, and the matter of unauthorized change to information has become very serious. Clever people can make minute or complex changes to data that can confuse or mislead those relying on the information. In one case in Illinois, a programmer changed all the passwords to a system controlling a production line, and then left the company. A worker in Detroit made very small changes to data in a system that delivered parts to a production line; the line gradually came to a halt, to the bewilderment of management. There have been innumerable incidents of students changing grades in school computers. Bank clerks have moved funds from one account to another or rounded all entries and moved the pennies into their own accounts. Opportunities to benefit from manipulation of data occur regularly to employees who are skilled in using systems that control valuable assets or monies. Fortunately, most employees are honest, but there are always a few who succumb to temptation.

The answer to unauthorized changes to electronic data must be a positive identification and authentication of everyone who creates a transaction in any system. Further, a log must record each action—what was done, when it was done, and who did it. This is a corollary to the "need to know" rule.

THE VIRUS SOFTWARE THREAT

In February 1985, Dr. Fred Cohen (then of Lehigh University) addressed the annual security workshop at a large corporation and demonstrated a virus software on a personal computer (PC) at the company's research center. This was one of the earliest recognitions that a potential security threat existed from clever software constructions, now known as "virus" software. At the time, most observers believed virus software to be an interesting technical exercise, but one that "really didn't apply to us."

A virus is a small program that has an "appending" capability; that is, the virus program can attach itself to any other program that meets certain specifications set by the writer of the virus. For example, almost all virus software checks to see if a program is already infected. Also, virus software will check to see that the virus can be appended only to an executable program (e.g., in MS-DOS, an .EXE or .COM program), since execution of the infected program generates reproduction and further distribution of the virus. Virus software often is delivered to an unsuspecting PC user in some misleading and attractive cover. (In this guise, the virus is a "Trojan Horse", but the terms are not synonymous.) It may be imbedded in a commercial software package normally costing hundreds of dollars but offered "free" on a hackers' network. Or it may be implanted in an attractive display or computer game. A clever virus is very difficult to identify; experts estimate four to six weeks of concentrated effort to find virus code in the average complex applications package.

Once attached to another program, the virus can reproduce itself when the host program is run, attaching itself to any other programs with which the infected program comes in contact. Thus the virus can spread through a system or network much like a physical virus can spread through a population of human carriers. The virus program may carry within itself certain instructions. These may be harmful, but they can also be beneficial or merely neutral. Consider the now-famous IBM Christmas virus. Its ostensible purpose was only to send a greeting to many people, but in doing so it overloaded the network by replicating itself on everyone's mail lists, thereby sending each user scores of similar greeting messages, until the network could no longer cope.

Other viruses have delivered Trojan horses, programs that look like friendly helpers, such as data compressors. But when run, the program may delete the disk directory, thereby making the disk and its contents useless to the computer user. Technical experts can see potential in using virus software to correct problems in networks. An early version of such software was the "worm" program developed and used at the Xerox Palo Alto Research Center in the early 1970s to fix a network problem. The virus did its job, but then it could not be shut off without extensive effort.

Experience with virus software attacks to 1990 shows that the virus software threat is real and has serious implications but that the actual risk at present is fairly remote. Consider that few virus attacks on commercial systems have been noted (the most famous, the IBM Christmas virus, is believed to have been a mistaken attempt to send a greeting, not sabotage). And, with few exceptions, no viruses have been found in public domain software. Rather, they have been distributed through commercial software packages (many of these were "pirated" or counterfeit copies passed around among university students). Finally, almost all attacks have occurred in the research and university environments (the Internet attack of 1988, for example), where the use of "free" software is common or where access is easy for many people. In such situations, people pass around floppy disks and exchange software freely, an ideal environment for spreading a "software plague."

Risks and Antidotes

With our current knowledge concerning potential virus software and methods of attack, very little can be done to *prevent* initiation of a virus software attack. (Positive protection against the virus threat would require major changes in the way computers are built and used, e.g., limited resources for users, no programming or compiling for anyone not defined as a programmer, limited transitivity, and limited sharing. Obviously, with the computers being developed and delivered today providing *increasing* user power, this will not happen soon.) If the virus attacker is clever, the attack will probably succeed to some degree. Internally initiated attacks, where the virus is introduced intentionally or unwittingly by an authorized user, appear to be the greatest risk at this time. A lesser risk is penetration through a network, perhaps from a secondary network. However, companies can take prudent steps to lessen risk and damage.

Risks from virus software attacks vary among types of systems and machines. Computer mainframes are considered to be relatively secure from virus attacks. Do not rule out an attack on a mainframe by a trusted insider, but consider that event unlikely because of the rigorous technical reviews, input, and program library controls as well as management overviews on software activity. Large networks are a moderate risk, not only from insiders or authorized outsiders but also from ubiquitous hackers. Significant numbers of PCs may be used; some may be connected to networks. Certain workstations have a dual personality; that is, they can run PC emulation on a network. These workstations and

PCs use MS-DOS, the environment posing the most severe risk. This is so because there is much software available, and it tends to be distributed through unauthorized copies and modified versions not attributable to identified authors.

Prudent information managers should consider the following six measures to help guard against catastrophic losses of information or compromises of information integrity due to virus attacks.

1.   Provide an awareness and training program, so that users of computers will know what a virus program is and will be be alert to symptoms of virus attacks. (A network user recently sent out a message to a large distribution saying "I have found this program that just says "BOOM." Does anyone know what it could be?" Such naiveté deserves the potential results.)

2.   Perform an analysis of exposure, so that managers will know what risks they may be accepting in choosing a course of action. Note that current risk analysis systems do not provide for handling the infectious characteristics of a virus attack, which may gradually extend over an entire company or network.

3.   Take reasonable precautions, including careful selection and testing of all new software and backup of files and operating systems. Current software "inoculation" packages may provide limited protection, but only against viruses already seen. Since there are an unlimited number of potential forms, the use of such packages is questionable in most situations.

4.   Ensure that computer users can reasonably recognize danger signs. Recognition allows the user to report suspicions and allows the company or agency to take action appropriate to the situation. Among signs of a virus attack are multiple, concurrent machine failures, unexplained increases in the amount of disk space occupied, and changes in the length of programs.

5.   Plan for a reaction to suspected "infection." The organization must be prepared to take action to isolate the suspected infected system(s) and to begin recovery through the use of stored backup copies of operating systems and data.

6.   Plan for recovery. By using backup tapes and disks, the system must be restarted in a "clean" state. The backup tapes and disks will be useless if they are not produced with reasonable frequency and kept for some significant time. A time-delay Trojan horse program could already be present on backup files when the virus attack becomes known.

Practical Suggestions

Security against virus software attacks may be viewed as having two stages:

- Strengthening the systems infrastructure to make it more robust, or healthy, so that it can recover from an attack
- Putting measures in place to minimize damages

Systems Robustness

All new programs must be thoroughly tested for quality and acceptability. This should be a function performed by some central agency, such as the data center quality control function or the information center. In most cases involving PCs, however, practical wisdom says that we will have to rely on individual users to test new software. Preferably, testing should extend over several weeks and should be done on an isolated system.

Public domain software (also known as shareware or freeware) should not be used unless obtained directly from the author, usually on payment of a small fee. Commercial software packages should be used only if obtained from reputable suppliers in sealed packages.

Preinstallation software quality checks should be performed at mainframe sites at installation of an application or operating system software. The data center should obtain, from the software supplier (the computer manufacturer in must cases), some method to ensure "certification" that the software delivered is clean and free from improper changes.

Minimizing Damages

All critical files should be backed up with a minimum of two versions. Operating systems software must be backed up on disk and stored securely, with release only when authorized.

Where the user deems it appropriate to the business situation, "inoculation" software should be installed. This may provide more psychological than actual protection, however, since the virus has so many potential forms.

THREE

Key Business Information Management Tasks

Imagine that you are the president of a wholesale automotive parts business. You ask your parts manager how many mufflers are in stock, and he says, "I don't know." Or imagine that you are the vice-president of materials for a steel mill and your customer wants to know if you have a certain type of steel on hand. You reply, "I have no way of finding out what is there." Or imagine that you are the comptroller of a large publishing company, and the vice-president of finance asks you how much cash the company has on hand. You reply, "We have never counted it."

These answers sound ridiculous. But we have shown information to be among the most critical (and expensive) resources of today's businesses, yet in most companies the information manager (if one exists) would not be able to answer these questions any more substantially.

If a company wishes to manage the information resource, it must begin by taking stock of its information base. It must manage information as it manages other resources. To get started, a company must identify the basic information elements needed to operate the business. Then management must assign values to each element so that it knows which are the elements it must control. Obviously, some public information (e.g., the weather report) may be needed but does not need to be conserved.

INFORMATION MANAGEMENT STRUCTURE

Before we discuss the details of getting control, let us consider an organization for managing information.

Information is very important, and the senior information executive should report directly to the CEO. It is important to recognize that this is not a systems job, although that function fits within the information manager's responsibilities. Rather, it is a broad responsibility for defining, developing, analyzing, processing, and delivering information to fit the business's needs and to contribute to business's profitability and growth through dynamic information uses. Through serendipitous analysis of current information systems opportunities and synergistic applications of information to business development, the information executive is placed to have a major effect on the company.

Herbert Halbrecht clearly defines the role of the information executive:

> He understands he is not managing technology as much as he is managing change, change of the decision making process as well as change in the way in which a company is run. He should be a participant in top management decisions from the outset, responsible for identifying the systems required as well as the cost of implementing these systems and their implications for an entire organization.[9]

The information executive really has the task of selling top management on the cost of and the opportunities arising from information. Within his or her responsibilities are a number of important tasks, including

1.   Identifying and controlling the business information base. (Technically, for computing purposes, this activity may be called *data administration,* but it is really a much broader function encompassing information in all forms.)

2.   Organizing the information elements so that business information processing and use are as efficient as possible. (Within technical computer use, this function is implemented through the "data dictionary.")

3.   Classifying information according to value, to allow appropriate control efforts (just as an inventory manager would spend more effort on a $10,000 assembly than on a $0.10 screw).

4.   Establishing and managing procedures to ensure the quality (reliability, integrity, and privacy) of critical (company classified) information.

This is a big job, and one fraught with risks. But there are risks in not doing anything, risks that competitors will gain an insurmountable advantage by using information better. Futurist author Alvin Toffler puts the case: "The next ten years contain the opportunity for the corporate computer executive to become obsolete. He is controlling dinosaurs while the ants are swarming over the world."[10] Toffler is speaking about traditional mainframe computing versus distributed computing and networks.

Figure 3.1 illustrates an information management organization. There is probably no "right" organization for information management, but key tasks must be addressed, and any suitable organization will be set up to meet those requirements.

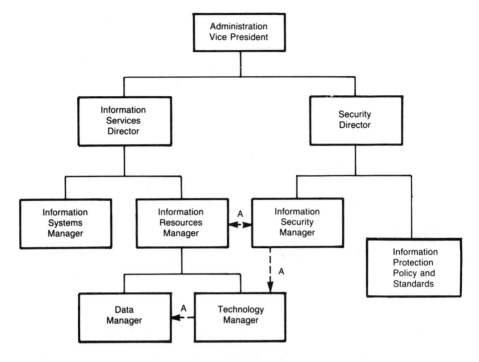

Figure 3.1   Information management organization. A, advisory.

IDENTIFYING AND CONTROLLING BUSINESS INFORMATION

Why should business managers care about the critical information elements used in business operations? Why not just go on assuming that information is free and that it can take care of itself?

Managers should be concerned because

- Without controls, information elements become duplicated in various systems and procedures, causing unnecessary expense and, even worse, errors and costly reprocessing.
- Unmanaged business information means casual development of nonstandardized information forms, making it impossible to compare data or to develop new applications systems using files from various departments; usually, these problems are "resolved" by creating more duplicative data files.
- Without management controls, middle- and lower-level managers can develop or demand unlimited numbers of information files or systems, increasing the cost of the information base.
- Unless some inventory of important information elements is undertaken and

maintained, management will be unlikely to recognize business opportunities offered by information on hand.

- Management cannot possibly know which information is really valuable or critical to business success unless it understands what constitutes the business information base.

The first task of the information executive, then, is to identify the information elements that make up the business information base. This will provide an inventory of data elements, a data element being the lowest or basic level of information. Typical business data elements are

Customer name and address

Product nomenclature and numbers

Supplier name and address

Employee name and address

General ledger accounts

Salespeople and commissions

There can be hundreds of such items. The key to data management is to establish one form for each element and then to ensure that whenever and wherever that element is used, only that one form is applied. At a very simple level, this should eliminate the old problem where a single customer is listed or recorded in various records or systems as John Smith & Co., Smith, John & Co., Smith Co., John Smith, John Smith Co., Smith Company, Smith & Co., and so forth, resulting in errors, confusion, duplicate billings, and similar expensive waste.

Information Ownership

Another benefit from an organization of business information results from controls over information use. This involves the concept of an "information owner." The information owner is the senior manager responsible for specified information elements. For example, the vice-president of personnel or a similar executive would be the information owner of all personnel information elements. As such, he or she would make decisions authorizing the use of personnel information elements and would also make information classification decisions indicating the level of protection required for such elements. Other functions should have similarly identified information owners, so that every information element in the company's information base is assigned to an owner. Without information owners, decisions to allow the use of information (and to incur significant expense) are made by default, typically by the information systems manager, which is an absurd situation. It is like allowing the company mechanic to decide who can use a company car.

Organizing Information Elements

Information elements must be organized properly, principally because of the widespread use of computers for virtually every move, processing, or delivery of information in business. This function is called data administration, and it is best done centrally so that all data use throughout the company can be as efficient and simple as possible. James Martin points out that

> At the highest level is the strategic planning of the data resources . . . the "data strategist," [who] is ultimately responsible for what files, data bases, and information resources exist. His staff may set data base policy and standards, evaluate and select software, determine what design tools are used, and maintain a corporate-wide inventory of data resources and a data dictionary.[11]

The data dictionary defines the company's data elements and indicates how the elements fit into technical database models. These models indicate how the information elements, in their standard forms, fit into the overall company information requirement, rather than the narrower view of, say, an individual programmer. (Recall that twenty years ago a system designer or application programmer made up information elements to fit his or her particular requirements. Each application had its own unique set of data files.)

Martin lists five questions concerning design and control of information systems in today's businesses (most using distributed processing through networks of computers).[12] These are as follows:

1. Where should database files be located (e.g., at headquarters or at a field location)?
2. How can integrity and synchronization be maintained?
3. How can conflicts be avoided?
4. Who designs data elements when several data owners are involved?
5. Who can enforce compatibility among systems and locations?

These are all data administration jobs. This book will not go into the technical details of data administration; however, information management today has many complex information organization and control issues to be resolved under the aegis of the information executive.

Classifying Valuable Information

Consider the decision process an individual goes through when he or she rents a safe deposit box. Logically, one first decides what items must be protected. This is a selective process; obviously, one cannot rent a box big enough to store everything one owns. We pick out the most critical or valuable items (analogous to the objective and subjective classification criteria) and store those in the box.

The same process applies to the company's information elements or combinations thereof, usually called records (when in electronic form) or documents. We must know which are valuable in themselves (subjective value) or must be safeguarded for legal or historical reasons (objective value). Most businesses will use more than one value level or classification. This is a decision of convenience; also, a company cannot afford to protect every valuable record or document as if it were critical; that would be too expensive. When a company does have a critical item, however, it would like to protect it accordingly. So a company usually assigns a number of different classifications, or values, to information.

Union Carbide Corporation developed an information classification and protection program in the mid-1980s after a careful survey of what other leading companies, including IBM Corporation, Xerox Corporation, and Eastman Kodak Company, were doing about information protection. The Union Carbide program is used here to illustrate an effective information classification scheme. The reader should realize that each company has unique requirements and information bases; his or her company probably should develop a classification scheme suitable to its particular business operations.

In the introduction to its classification and protection booklet, Union Carbide says

> This Program is designed to improve the care, custody and control of Company information which if lost or misused could adversely affect UCC operations, employees, customers, or stockholders. It provides guidelines for identifying this information, and regulations for protecting it against loss, theft, misuse, or improper disclosure.

Note that this statement refers to what will be protected and who will be protected, identifies valuable information, and includes procedures for information safeguarding. It describes the company's classification program in a nutshell.

An accompanying Policy statement says

> Company information will be protected by measures commensurate with its nature. A system of information classification, with appropriate protection regulations, will be implemented throughout the Corporation.

Management's intent could not be more clearly stated.

At Union Carbide, three classifications are defined:

1.   Category 1: UCC general. This category includes company information that is not particularly sensitive or confidential, is not covered by a secrecy agreement, is not required to be legally protected by UCC as confidential, and thus requires discretionary but not confidential treatment. It is the corporation's property, and discretion must be exercised to avoid its loss, misuse, or improper disclosure. Examples are miscellaneous correspondence, transaction documents, invoices, and cancelled checks.

2. Category 2: UCC business confidential. This category includes company information that is confidential, sensitive, or both. Such information must be made available only to individuals with the need and the right to know. (This last sentence refers to a key principle, the need to know, on which any information control program is based.) Generally, examples of this classification are any employee information that, if misused or improperly disclosed, could violate an individual's rights of privacy.

3. Category 3: UCC registered confidential. This category includes company information that is highly confidential, of the utmost sensitivity, or both. Because of its nature, it must be closely controlled and accounted for from creation to destruction. Such information must be made available only to specific individuals who have the need and the right to know. Examples are strategic business data, highly controversial information, and sensitive preannouncement data.

Observation of the information security regulations and procedures of a number of progressive companies leads one to recognize a general rule:

- High-value (classification) information is restricted to a specifically identified group of employees.
- Middle-value (classification) information is restricted to a class of employees with a need to know.
- Low-value (classification) information is private to the company and not to be released to outsiders.

Union Carbide gives the following instruction to the originators of information (in the classic case, this would be the information owners):

> The criteria for assessing the sensitivity and confidentiality of Company information, and hence its classification, will be the detrimental impact of its loss, misuse, or improper disclosure upon (a) the Corporation's financial performance; (b) the orderly conduct of Company business; or (c) UCC's employees, customers, or stockholders. In all cases, information should be assigned to the least restrictive category which is consistent with these criteria.

Effective protection of information relies on correct classification. This, in turn, depends on the knowledge and awareness of many employees, who in the course of their daily work must be motivated to take the time to obtain, determine, and assign a classification and then to mark the record or document accordingly. Further, all these employees must be ready and willing to observe the appropriate protective measures suitable to any given classification. This is a tall order, and we shall discuss the implementation and maintenance of effective programs in Part III.

ESTABLISHING INFORMATION QUALITY

As discussed earlier, information quality refers to the characteristics of reliability, integrity, and privacy. How do managers, and specifically the information executive, ensure that the business does indeed have quality information? A number of practical management actions support quality information:

1. Careful management of the information resource, already described
2. Careful design, development, and implementation of information procedures and systems, with a constant view toward the long-range business strategic goals, always seizing opportunities for synergistic benefits
3. Thorough employee training coupled with expert supervision and motivation, along with effective controls, to reduce errors and eliminate opportunities (or perceived opportunities) for fraud or mischief
4. Appropriate security and contingency measures suitable to information classification and tailored to the business's operational activities

Information Management

The term *information management* is a broad one. In this context it refers to responsibilities for

- Optimizing benefits and minimizing overall costs to the business for providing useful information as needed to make good decisions and to increase profits
- Organizing information elements used in the business to give optimal support to the above
- Providing technology applications so that the business will realize benefits from its information, beyond mere need-to-know data, in a timely and efficient manner.

We have already discussed some of these managerial tasks. Paul Strassmann emphasizes this role when he says "the successful adaptation of information technology requires agents of change—the high-performance individuals—who lead an organization in accepting a transformed workplace."[13] The information resource manager should be such an agent for change.

Design and Implementation of Efficient Procedures and Systems

There is little doubt that, so far, information technology and business systems experts have failed to deliver to business management what is needed. But there is hope. Better programming methods and languages (even COBOL can be done better), improved realization of the complex relationship between system designer and system user, more powerful fourth-generation user-oriented retrieval languages, high-powered database microcomputers, efficient networks, data center management tools, and other recent developments offer the chance to identify and provide exceptional information systems. Manual information procedures are also important and must not be overlooked.

The information executive will supervise an employee responsible for operational information systems. The role of this job is developing to include data and voice network management in addition to the traditional systems development and data processing responsibilities. This technical job is a vital one if maximum benefit is to be gained from the business's investment in information. The task here is to deliver the right information systems at the right time. Probably the hardest part is to sort out those technologies most appropriate to business information needs.

Performance of Knowledge Workers

The most serious challenge to quality information is the careless errors employees make. Although well-designed systems may catch some errors before serious damage is done, significant losses will occur. Bad decisions will be made, a product will be lost or shipped to the wrong address, orders will be filled incorrectly, employees will be paid too much or too little, customers will be provided erroneous data, too much or too little product will be produced, and so on.

The performance of employees dealing with information (knowledge workers) relates directly to three things:

1. The systems they are provided, how simple and clear their procedures are, how well the controls work, and how efficient the forms and tools are.
2. How well the employees are trained for the tasks they must do. It is important that people understand how they fit in. In 1968, Sealtest Foods was having problems with an ice cream billing system. The data center was in New York, but the ice cream plant was in Massachusetts. The data center supervisory staff took a day off to visit with the ice cream factory employees. Many problems were resolved during that visit, when each "side" came to understand the other's procedures.
3. The quality of supervision and motivation. Good supervisors can make a poorly designed system work. Poor supervisors can cause even the best of systems to be beset with problems. At a data center in Paris, the data entry supervisor admitted she had no idea where the forms came from or where data went once they were entered. No wonder there were problems.

The operation of many information procedures is probably outside the information executive's authority, but his or her responsibility extends to seeing to it that well-designed systems are properly installed and that installation includes employee training.

Information Security and Contingency Planning

If, as we have seen, information is a key business asset, then a company rightly should want to protect it and to make contingency plans should it not be available despite its best efforts. Providing effective protection for a company's classified information is not just a means for keeping the information private and available. It is necessary should a business have to go to court to prove ownership.

In a well-known case, *Motorola vs. Fairchild Camera and Instrument Corporation* (D. Arizona 1973, 366 F. Supp. 1173), the court said that the original owner has lost rights to data because it had failed to

- Set up a program of information protection
- Identify which data were valuable
- Implement the program though regular employee protective practices

Information security and contingency planning involves all three forms of information—mental, written, and electronic—and includes document marking and handling, computer hardware and software, contractual agreements with employees, contractors, and suppliers, and plans to recover business capabilities should an information loss occur. These topics are covered thoroughly in Part II. Here, suffice it to say this is a major information management responsibility.

Information management is a critical, high-level responsibility. It consists of a number of complex, interrelated tasks with technologic overtones. The information executive should be a key confidant of top management, since information may well be the key to business success.

PART II

How to Identify, Evaluate, and Protect Critical Information Elements

FOUR

Classifying Valuable
Business Information

It is a truism that a company cannot protect everything effectively. In all cases, it must determine what information is the most valuable and then take reasonable steps to protect that particular item. In some cases, a careful analysis of what is really important can provide better security and reduce the cost of security.

In the 1960s, the U.S. Strategic Air Command decided that having guards and fences around its air bases was a waste of time. Every attempt at penetration by those responsible for testing such things showed that fences keep out only one's friends. The U.S. Strategic Air Command then decided to place guards around the important things—airplanes, hangars, critical supplies—and not worry about people coming over the fences. This worked well and actually increased the level of security where it was really needed; it also saved money.

For the information resource, a company must take a similar approach. It must identify critical pieces of information and then follow a well-planned program for protecting those items. Classification of information is the first step in this process.

NOMENCLATURE FOR CLASSIFICATION

Probably only about 10% of all information in a typical business should be classified. Of this, less than 1% of all information should be at the highest classification level. This is information that would be available to only a few specified people and that usually would be kept locked in a safe or encrypted for electronic storage or communication. The remaining 9% of all information would be classified at a medium level and should be restricted to groups of employees needing it to do their jobs. Finally, all information regarding employee records, medical records, and applicant records should be classified to ensure privacy.

41

The first task is to identify information that should fall into one of these classifications. Although this is always a matter of judgment, a set of guidelines is necessary to maintain reasonable consistency in classification decisions. Keep in mind that classification decisions will be made by many people in widely varying circumstances; although responsibility for classification rests with the information owner, practical business operation indicates that these decisions be made on the spot by the information originator, probably following instructions set up by the information owner within company policy.

For example, the guidelines for classifying information might be:

- *Registered* (highest classification). This includes information that, if improperly disclosed, could cause serious damage to company operations. An example is information concerning product strategy or product-related research.
- *Private* (middle classification). This includes information that, if improperly disclosed, could have a substantially detrimental effect on company operations. An example is customer lists, which would be of value to a competitor.
- *Personal* (special classification). This is information that an individual might find embarrassing or detrimental if improperly exposed. Examples are personnel and medical records.

These definitions do not mention information retention or legal requirements, which also should be addressed through classification. However, they do illustrate practical guidelines for people who must make information classification decisions.

Note here that government classifications should always be kept separate from company classifications; the government nomenclature (top secret, secret, confidential) should never be used for company business. It is a good idea always to use the company name (e.g., IBM classified) when referring to company classified information to avoid confusion. Such designation would be helpful later, in event of a lawsuit. It shows that the information was important to the company and also was protected by them, thus giving it value in the eyes of the court.

Experience has shown that two or three classification types are probably appropriate and manageable for most businesses. These should have descriptive titles that indicate their relative importance. Some titles currently used by various companies are

- Highest level: registered confidential, registered, restricted
- Middle level: private, business confidential, business private
- Lowest level: general, company general

CLASSIFICATION PHILOSOPHY

Information should be classified to represent business requirements for information security and availability and to meet legal requirements. These requirements fall into two categories:

1. Objective classification, relating to requirements outside the information itself. Generally, these requirements concern information retention and conservation, most frequently required by law or for historical purposes. This classification is typically marked "retention schedule X," with the "X" being a number referring to a list showing requirements.
2. Subjective classification, relating to the information itself. Generally, these requirements concern the company's need to keep the information private. The business privacy requirement is usually divided into three information groupings:
    a. Information restricted to a small group of individuals specified, when the information is developed, by the originator or by top management. This is the highest classification.
    b. Information restricted to a group of employees, not usually specified by name, who require the information to perform assigned tasks. This is the middle-level classification. Special subjective classification, e.g., medical records, falls within this group.
    c. All other business information, which may not be released to outsiders without management approval (typically, the information owner—the executive responsible for that particular information element).

MAKING CLASSIFICATION DECISIONS

Subjective classification decisions are made in two ways:

*   By the information owner
*   On the spot

The information owner specifies that certain classes or types of information will always be classified at a certain level. For example, the vice-president of marketing determines that customer lists for a given territory will always be classified as *company confidential* and that the general customer list (for the entire company) will be classified as *registered*.

Because critical or valuable information will be developed by various managers and executives for whom it is impractical or inconvenient to contact the information owner, classification decisions must be made on the spot when information is first developed, either in written or electronic form. This means that all employees must have training about the methodology of making classification decisions and about their individual responsibilities.

Objective classifications are usually made following published company instructions for records retention or concerning legal requirements. Some documents could have two classifications, one a subjective classification indicating inherent value, and the other an objective classification indicating retention requirements. In practice, these cases are few.

Although most classification decisions are made manually, that is, by an individual creating a document or record, computer systems could be designed to assign classifications automatically by comparing a subject against a stored subject classification list. Note that classification indications, either in the form of an indicator flag or a graphics image, should be a permanent part of any company computer records. These should be marked both internally, with an electronic or logical label, and externally, with a paper label or stamp.

Guidelines for Determining Correct Classification

Proper information classification is essential for efficient (cost-effective) protection. The correct classification results when

1. People understand the purpose of classification
2. People have a clear set of guidelines in making classification decisions

A set of three Classification Indicators (courtesy Digital Equipment Corporation) may be suggested to guide employees in determining the correct classification for various information items. These indicators can be adapted to any classification scheme or classification titles.

Classification Indicators

There are three primary classification decision indicators:

1. *How many people are authorized* to have this information?
2. *How valuable* is this information?
3. *How sensitive* is this information?

The following categories illustrate the application of the classification indicators. (Each indicator question is followed by an answer (A), with the correct classification value for that reply.)

First indicator: How many people are authorized to have this information?

A. Only those on a list identified by the originator. Classification: HIGH VALUE
A. Only those employees in a group, project, department, or function having a need to know the information. Classification: MIDDLE VALUE
A. All employees. Classification: LOW VALUE (may include all unclassified information)

Second indicator: What is the value of this information?

A. In the hands of a competitor, it could severely impact the ability to successfully market a product, complete a business arrangement, or succeed in a business strategy. Classification: HIGH VALUE
A. In the hands of a competitor, it could compromise competitive posture, reveal sales strategies, reveal engineering or software developments, or similar information. Classification: MIDDLE VALUE
A. In the hands of a competitor, it could provide a piece of information that, when added to other pieces, may reveal business strategy, sales plans, or similar information. Classification: LOW VALUE

Third indicator: How sensitive is this information?

A. If revealed publicly or to competitors, the information owner could be subject to lawsuits, seriously embarrassed, or placed in an untenable position. Classification: HIGH VALUE
A. If revealed to outsiders, secret plans could be exposed, resulting in a compromise of business strategy. Classification: MIDDLE VALUE
A. If revealed to outsiders, information could provide clues to employee assignments, product plans, customer lists, and similar routine business data. Classification: LOW VALUE

It is not possible to describe all the various reports, memos, subject matters, etc., that should be classified. Therefore, the illustrative titles given with these indicators should be used only as a general guide for the learned judgment of the information originator, or in the case of an application system, the information owner.

The classification indicators should be used collectively, whenever practical, to strengthen the validity of the classification decision. Please note that personal information, that is, data that an individual would normally wish to remain private, is a special case and usually falls into the HIGH VALUE category.

As a general rule, *all* business information should be private to the company, whether classified or not.

Classification Logos or Fonts

Marking documents or electronically displayed records requires special fonts or logos. Merely using the words *company classified* is not sufficient. The markings should be big and bold enough to bring to any observer's attention the fact that "this document is *company classified*." Some appropriate classification logos in use display a keyway symbol, a lock, and a key. Figure 4.1 illustrates some examples.

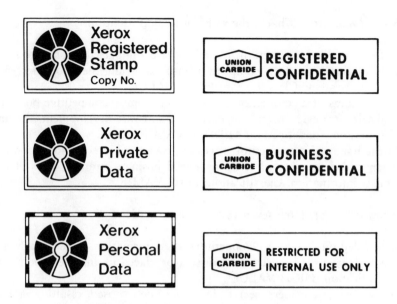

Figure 4.1   Classification logos.

If a document or computer display record is prepared on equipment that cannot handle graphics, and use of a stamp or dry transfer is impractical, such as on some computer printers, the rules should provide an alternative. One suggestion is to type the classification nomenclature in capital letters surrounded by asterisks, as follows:

```
**************
* RESTRICTED *
**************
```

Keep in mind that this practice should be an exception, never the rule! Official classification logos should be mandatory.

Arguing Against Information Classification

People often say, "Why mark something valuable—that just shows the bad guys what to steal." Their position sounds reasonable but is not based on solid experience or law. Major companies with notable success in competitive environments have found information classification marking to be a necessity. They have found that without classification marking, nothing is protected. And they know that to prove ownership of information in court, they must show a real effort to identify valuable data. Classification marking is the answer.

Classification: Too Much or Too Little?

Correct use of the classification scheme is important to protect valuable information. Some people, however, see classification as a means to indicate their importance or to increase their prestige.

Overclassification dilutes the effect of the protection effort; it creates masses of classified information that can become so common as to cause protection rules to be disregarded entirely. Underclassification may leave important information unprotected and thus risk exposure that could harm the company.

The information executive must maintain some surveillance over the entire classification program to ensure that the general intent is being followed. The information owners must make sure that the selected employees who regularly handle or process particular information are given practical guidelines on what and what not to classify.

Company auditors can check on classification effectiveness when they do their regular reviews of business operations. Continuing employee awareness efforts, booklets, and posters help to keep the classification program a practical one in consonance with business requirements and operating practices.

INFORMATION END OF LIFE

Most information has a fairly short value period. Within a few months, and certainly within a few years, most information has lost all but historical value. It is a good idea to set classification expiration dates or periods for company classified information. This can be done as a standard practice, set out in policy, or done by stamping high-value documents with an expiration or declassification date. This allows more reasonable destruction practices for records retention purposes and reduces the cost of secure storage for long-term documents and computer records.

Classification is the key to protecting business information. It must be carefully planned and meticulously implemented if the effort is to succeed. The information executive and functional information owners have important roles in getting a program started and maintained.

FIVE

Using Classification to Manage and Protect Information

Classification is a tool. It tells employees what to do with information that has been appropriately marked. By following the information-handling procedures for the indicated classification, the employee provides appropriate protection and, by so doing, establishes the company's legal rights to the information.

Later in this chapter we will consider some proved procedures for protecting and controlling valuable business information. There are no doubt other ways to do these tasks. The manager should define information protection requirements in the way that best suits the company's needs, both for business operating efficiency and for information protection. An illustrative information security standard is provided in the Appendixes, showing a complete set of procedures.

The procedures used to protect information follow from the company classification assigned to that information. In many instances, the first step is the act of determining the level of classification. We will follow such a process in an imaginary company, the ABC Corporation, which grows and sells specialized ocean plant life developed through genetic engineering technologies.

HANDLING INFORMATION

High-Value Information

Daniel James is a biologist who has been working with aquacultural experiments to develop more efficient ways to feed crustaceans. James believes he has found an important and novel new form of plant for this purpose. He has just completed writing a report to the ABC chief scientist concerning this discovery, using his microcomputer word processing system.

When James was hired, he was shown a videotape concerning ABC Corporation's program for protecting proprietary information. In addition, he received a booklet containing ABC's information handling regulations. So James gets out his booklet, since he remembers that he is supposed to protect information with potential product value, and looks up definitions of ABC's information classifications. The instructions say that any new research results that could have product implications must be classified as ABC *registered*, the highest company classification. The chief scientist has the authority to assign classifications for research results, but he is away on a business trip, and James must make the decision now, on his own. To wait would risk exposing the document he has produced.

From the microcomputer system's font file, James retrieves the ABC *registered* logo and places it electronically at the top of his report. At the same time, the system sets a flag on the computer record that will indicate, to any other ABC systems, that this is a *registered* document that must be handled in special ways.

James now sends the document to a printer. The printer will not produce the printed paper until James arrives and enters his password. The flagged file sees to that. When James retrieves the document from the printer, having entered his password, the ABC *registered* logo is printed very noticeably at the top.

At ABC, all research documents are maintained in a special library. James takes the original document to the library and has a copy made. From now on, no one will be able to get a copy of the document from any source other than the library. James, or any other ABC employee, is not permitted to make additional copies of ABC *registered* documents.

Knowing he will be attending a company meeting out of town in a week, James informs the librarian. The librarian will send a numbered copy to the out-of-town ABC office, and James will pick it up there. ABC *registered* documents are not permitted to be carried off company premises.

Should James wish to send the report electronically over ABC's networks, the communications server in the network at the laboratory will recognize the security flag and will encrypt (or encode, using a complex algorithm) the information before sending it over telecommunications circuits outside company premises.

Finally, James locks the report away in a cabinet with a bar and padlock.

Now, if you have never used an information classification system, you may be saying to yourself, "What a lot of bother." It is true some detail must be attended to, but the procedure James followed is in use by highly successful companies in competitive businesses. A number of companies have been destroyed when, after their critical information had been stolen, they discovered they had no redress in court because they had also thought protection was too much bother.

Middle-Value Information

Paul Thomas is the comptroller for ABC Corporation. Most of the financial reports and analyses he deals with are company classified at the middle level, called ABC *restricted*. Reports are locked away in desks when not in use or when the user is away from his or her workstation for more than one hour.

When a systems consultant is hired to develop analytic tools for microcomputers, Thomas makes sure the consultant has signed a disclosure agreement, to protect ABC in the event the consultant gains access to confidential information.

Thomas regularly checks his subordinates' information-handling practices and regularly walks through copy rooms after working hours to check on documents left behind. (Although copiers are a wonderful tool for the industrial spy, the worst exposure is from copies of documents inadvertently left in copiers by faithful secretaries and picked up by maintenance or cleaning workers or casual passersby.)

Thomas also insists that all sensitive accounting reports be clearly marked (stamped or computer printed) with the ABC *restricted* logo. His interest in securing information has made the accounting department an example to other areas of the company. Accounting employees know that information is not to be shared with other employees on the basis of curiosity or casual request, but only if the person has a true need to know. Since the daily routine of work is almost always with the same set of people, this is not a big problem. Requests for information from outside the working group must be approved by Thomas.

Personnel Information

Personnel or human resources information (including medical records) is often handled as a special classification. Generally, the rules concerning personnel information reflect the individual's normal desire to have certain facts held private. In some jurisdictions, privacy laws establish hard and fast rules concerning the handling and protection of personnel records. Certain European countries have laws that require strict recordkeeping so that employee records custodians can prove who has been given access to such data.

Secretaries and others outside the personnel function should be made to understand that any handling or processing of personnel records must be done in strict confidence. A company classification (such as ABC *personal data*) is needed for marking, and in some cases a cover sheet is appropriate.

As a rule, personnel information is available only to the servicing personnel function, the immediate supervisor, and the employee concerned. Computer records are protected by access control systems, and all computer records have the correct logo and warning flag. Usually, the company classification for personnel records is determined and permanently assigned, when the information management program is implemented, by the information executive and the senior personnel manager.

SPECIAL SITUATIONS

When networks of computers are used, information can be transferred to or among groups of people with lightning speed. Special arrangements and care are thus needed, usually wherever professionals work. Engineering, manufacturing, research, financial analysis, and strategy planning are business functions that today are highly automated.

Such systems should provide for security controls that are easy to use. Every user should be identifiable; every action, auditable. Password changes should be simple to make and encouraged, if not enforced, by the system. When high-value information is regularly processed, users should be able to call an encryption routine for data to be transmitted outside the facility or stored on removable disks.

Screen displays and printing facilities should have convenient graphics to show the company information protection logos when needed. When security logos are set, the system should also set a flag on the file or document to indicate special handling to the various parts of the network. Distribution (electronic mail) systems should have built-in security features to control the use of distribution lists or broadcast mailings when a security flag is set on a file or document.

Of course, stored data files should have security protection; this is true even if the information is not company classified. Too often, people with technical skills can browse through a network and pick up enough bits and pieces of information to make a reasonably correct analysis of management's plans, product strategy, and so forth. And, with today's vast interconnected networks, the people browsing may well be unknown and unauthorized outsiders.[2]

CLASSIFICATION REQUIRES JUDGMENT

Determining the most suitable classification for a given information item is a matter for learned judgment. Initially, when an information management program is begun, the information executive and the information owner cooperatively determine the proper classification for basic information elements and for routine, regularly produced reports or files. Examples of information items that should probably have fixed company classifications are customer lists, employee records, and monthly accounting reports. In most cases, the classifications established in the initial process can be programmed into the computer systems that produce these reports and the classification logos automatically applied at printing time. When reports or other documents are typewritten, the classification markings are usually stamped onto the document in prescribed ways (e.g., top and bottom of each page, front and back pages).

A more difficult situation occurs later, when in the course of business operations a manager or professional who is neither the information executive nor the information owner must make a classification decision. The decision must be made promptly and with good judgment. This is crucial if the information is to be properly classified and protected.

In a certain case in New York, a manager delayed making a classification decision, wanting to ask his boss about it. In the meantime, his secretary made copies for the addressees he had indicated. One of those people, not realizing the importance of the information, made further copies, and one got into the hands of a local gossip reporter. The information was in the newspaper the next day, with resultant embarrassment and turmoil.

The lesson here is that any information management program must become well understood, and every employee (perhaps except for production workers) must understand the purpose and methods involved. Everyone must be motivated to follow the procedures, which means management support is essential.

Classification is essential to information control and protection. Making classification decisions requires learned judgment based on knowledge of the purposes and methods of the company's information management system and its classification scheme. Workers using information as "material" must be both aware and motivated to make proper classification decisions and to follow up with appropriate security measures based on published requirements. Without such measures there can be no quality information.

SIX

Trade Secrets, Copyrights, and Matters of Law

Any company information considered to be of value (proprietary), and hence worth protecting through legal means, must be both useful and not publicly known. The terms *proprietary information* or *intellectual property* are interchangeable and are often used to describe information private to, and important to, a business. The important information on which a business is based may be technical, that is, explaining how to do or make something, or general, including customer lists or lists of prospects.

Knowing what important proprietary information exists is a necessary first step to establishing legal rights. The information element identification and classification process (identifying the business information base) is a way to do this; this process was discussed earlier, in the section on implementation of information management.

Establishing ownership of technical information developed in the course of business requires employee contracts that clearly state that any ideas coming from the employee's work belong to the company. Such contracts should be used generally for any high-technology business and, in special situations (e.g., scientists, engineers, chefs), for any business.

SELECTING FROM LEGAL PROTECTION ALTERNATIVES

Legal protection alternatives are useful in some cases for protecting company information, but the business itself must also take reasonable actions to recognize value and make an effort at protection.

Patent

A patent is an exclusive right to use an idea that is both new (hence the patent search necessary before granting) and useful. The owner of a patent does not particularly care if the idea is exposed, since he or she has exclusive rights to it under law for a limited time. In fact, the very act of patenting exposes the idea, because it is published by the U.S. Patent Office. So, in some cases, a company may decide not to use a patent but rather to rely on trade secret practices (see below).

Patents are expensive to obtain, and extensive delays may be encountered in the process. After a patent is granted, enforcing one's rights may be very difficult. A product may look like the one a company has patented, but it may be next to impossible to prove that it has been manufactured in the some way.

A court may invalidate a patent if a similar previous invention, also patented, is discovered. The second company might also be cited for infringement.

Trade Secret

Information qualifies as a trade secret and can be defended as such in court if the company has identified the material as valuable and secret, has set up a system for identifying and protecting such material, and has required that its employees actually follow this protection system. The value of a trade secret depends on the profits it produces; a secret that has never produced profits may not be considered to have any value and hence may not be protected by law. There are still risks, however. Someone outside the company could independently discover the same information. (If they also keep it a secret, it can be shared in secret, and the legal protection still applies.) The information could be exposed through carelessness. Security could be ineffective or insufficient.

One advantage a patent has over a trade secret involves the licensing of a process or technology. The licensee probably would feel more secure if the information were patented; the patent provides a clear legal right, while trade secrets are always open to a challenge in court.

Copyright

A copyright protects the arrangement of certain information, not the information itself. Music, for example, consists of an arrangement of a common set of notes. The notes can be used by anyone, but the arrangement of the notes in a copyrighted score makes the particular piece private property. Copyright can be claimed by the originator of a work simply by indicating the copyright symbol, ©, the year of origination, and the name of the claimant. Copyrighted materials can be registered with the U.S. Copyright Office, thereby allowing suits to be brought in defense.

A copyright has advantages over trade secrets in certain cases. A copyright is an absolute reservation of privilege to a specified person or company, but a trade secret implies that others may know of the information and share it. The issue of business strategy versus copyright or trade secret protection for information is a complex one, and experienced legal counsel is needed.

PRACTICAL APPLICATION

Most businesses choose to use trade secret law as the basis for protecting valuable business information. This is the basis for the information classification program discussed earlier. James Pooley, in his excellent reference work *The Executive's Guide to Protecting Proprietary Business Information and Trade Secrets,* suggests that information protection has three goals:[14]

1. To prevent theft
2. To discourage theft by establishing the value of the trade secrets and the difficulty of stealing them, as well as the fact that any unauthorized user will face prosecution
3. To maximize the appearance of the program as one designed to meet the first two goals

We can accomplish these goals by

- Establishing an information management program to identify the company's critical information
- Classifying such information to indicate value
- Setting up information management practices ensuring protection through regular, required employee actions involving proper marking and handling of valuable information.

In the landmark case *Motorola vs. Fairchild Camera and Instrument Corp.,* which invalidated Motorola's claims for trade secret protection, the judge noted that "there were no signs in the area warning of trade secrets, no warnings given to those taking tours, and no statement requiring nondisclosure agreements required to be signed or acknowledged." He further pointed out that outsiders could see, time, and operate the "secret" machines and even observe a "secret" process through a microscope. Thus, although Motorola had given lip service to trade secret protection, its failure to set up and operate a procedure for protecting the information denied it the protection of law.

If a business wishes to protect its proprietary information, it must take prudent and careful actions in a consistent manner. That means a well-conceived information protection program. The policy and information standards in the Appendixes illustrate such a program.

INFORMATION LIABILITY

Today we see the lawsuit being used as a remedy for just about anything. Companies that process information, even if only their own information, are potential defendants in court should an information error or careless handling result in a perception of damage by an individual or by another company. Peter Marx, chief counsel of the Information Industry Association, says that

> Most companies today, in their daily business, are part of what you might call an "information chain." And that means that a major part of their business involves taking information from a variety of sources, doing a variety of things to it—such as manipulating it using a computer—and either using it to gain a competitive edge, selling it, or passing it on in same way.[15]

Confusing, erroneous, or misunderstood information can lead information users to make wrong decisions. Exposed information can result in embarrassment or loss of opportunity. The company that processed, provided, or relied on such information can find itself in court.

This "information liability" means that businesses must make sure they have well-designed and well-controlled information resources—in other words, quality information. And in all aspects of the information management effort, good legal advice is needed.

Advantageous aspects of the law should not be missed by management. Criminal actions may be possible against the perpetrator of information theft. If employees and outsiders know that a company intends to prosecute whenever possible, they may be dissuaded from acting against that company's interests. Of course, a well-founded information control program forms the basis for successful prosecution.

Bottom and Gallati report a case at 3M Company, where an employee agreed to go to work for another company at a substantial pay increase, provided he would bring with him certain 3M secrets. He turned over ten formulas and then resigned from 3M, explaining he was going to work for a company that was not a competitor.[16]

Various forms of legally binding agreements can be used to strengthen the company's case. These include disclosure agreements, covenants promising not to engage in competitive activities for a certain period (these require special care, since courts generally hold them to be restrictive covenants), and agreements to disclose to the company any discoveries or inventions during employment.

Many legal means are available to help companies protect their valuable information. However, they do not operate automatically, since in every case the company must take actions to establish information rights and to be able to demonstrate an effort to provide information evaluation and protection.

PART III

Effective Programs for Information Management

SEVEN

A Structure
for Managing
Information Security

Effective management of a function always requires a common understanding, among the managers and functions involved, of *definitions* of the tasks at hand. A set of accepted definitions concerning the various aspects of information security is essential. Precise definition of information security terminology allows us to specify responsibility and to direct efforts clearly in securing all information forms. Some sample definitions are suggested in the following section.

DEFINITIONS FOR INFORMATION SECURITY*

Information security The process of ensuring that all information (that is, all information created during company business operations including engineering, manufacturing, marketing, and other processes) is appropriately protected

All information Refers to information in all three forms: paper or microforms; electronic (digital, analog [includes voice and fax], etc.); and mental (the employee knowledge base, addressed through employment and other contracts)

Appropriately Refers to a process of management risk acceptance and the assignment of relative information value through classification

Management risk acceptance Refers to senior management guidance, from decisions based on risk analysis and other data, concerning the investments considered appropriate to information protection, generally or in specific cases of information sets or applications

Assignment of relative values Refers to the decision made by the originator (or owner, in the case of a systems application) of an information item or set, concerning the appropriate digital classification, and hence the protection effort to

---

*Courtesy: Digital Equipment Corporation

be expended for that item or set. Information security policy and standards specify the definitions and protections for each classification.

Network security   The protection of the company's networks and connected resources. Network security is necessary for, and is a subset of, information security. Network security does not, by itself, ensure information security.

Computer security   The protection of the operations and data in process in a computing system, usually via the operating system controls. Computer security is necessary for, and is a subset of, information security. When computers are a part of a network, computer security is a necessary subset of network security. Computer security does not necessarily ensure information security.

Application security   The protection of the processes and data provided by instructions in an application system. It may consist of security controls separate from, or relying upon, computer security.

Document security   The protection of paper forms of information via proper handling and marking processes. A subset of information security, document security does not, by itself, ensure information security.

RESPONSIBILITY FOR INFORMATION SECURITY

Ask almost any business executive, "Who manages your information resource?" and you will hear (1) "I don't know," (2) "We have never thought about it," or (3) "The systems manager." The same executives will know immediately who manages financial resources, who manages personnel resources, and who manages inventories.

In survey results published in August 1987, *Computerworld* reported that fewer than 15% of banks, 8% of financial services businesses, and 15% of manufacturing businesses have invested in encryption or port control systems for their networks.[17] Such data indicate that most companies have not bothered to manage information, although most managers realize that information is valuable and important to business success. They seem to prefer to take the risk of information exposure or loss rather than make a prudent effort to control it.

The poor systems manager gets blamed for all sorts of things, some of which are properly his or her responsibility, but many of which are not of his or her doing. Add to this the idea that a systems manager can somehow manage information. All the systems manager really does is process information. We would be just as illogical if we held the production manager responsible for inventory of raw and finished materials!

Most critical information is on paper for a part of its working life. Writing in *Computer & Communications Decisions*, Cathy Dingman points out that

Advances in printing technology have made it easy to forget the dream of replacing paper with electronic documents. . . . For all the talk about local area networks and micro to mainframe links, corporations haven't implemented them widely enough to begin even thinking about replacing paper as the medium of choice.[18]

The systems manager simply has no handle on controlling the paper blizzard; that is a task that must be assigned—a part of information management responsibility—if the information asset is to be managed.

Although information systems (almost always involving computers these days, but also including manual procedures) are an essential part of information management, they are not the same as information management. Rather, the responsibility for managing information is a broad, high-level responsibility involving strategic planning.

Among other interesting stories in his book *Innovation and Entrepreneurship*, Peter F. Drucker tells about Macy's insistence on fashion merchandising as its lead department when in reality the market was changing.[19] Bloomingdale's, on the other hand, analyzed its customers' profiles and recognized that customer interest in appliances indicated a changing demand. As a result of having better information, Bloomingdale's became "the New York store," while Macy's suffered a temporary decline.

Information is too important to be "left alone." Management must put a structure in place to ensure its control.

CONCEPTS AND APPLICATIONS: THE THREE-DIMENSIONAL MATRIX

A security program for computer-processed business information may be envisioned as a three-dimensional matrix. The three planes of the matrix consist of

- Front plane—the three levels of directives:
  1. Executive program direction (policy)
  2. Program management (standards)
  3. Operating management (local procedure)
- Side plane—the four levels of protection:
  1. Physical protection
  2. Procedural protection
  3. Logical protection
  4. Transformation protection (usually encryptions)
- Top plane—information user groups having protection requirements, usually differing among organizations:
  1. Business management systems
  2. Research and engineering
  3. Office automation and personal computing
  4. Manufacturing systems
  5. Timesharing, distributed processing, and distributed computing
  6. Data processing and telecommunications

Figure 7.1 illustrates the program matrix.

Levels of directive are established to allow flexibility in dealing with varying requirements and situations in a large business. In addition, the lower levels of directive permit management to cope with the nuances of technology.

Levels of protection refer to the grouping of security elements by physical, procedural, logical, and transformational classes. This arrangement allows the system designer to select from among a menu of security alternatives to choose the best (most economical?) array of security protection measures for any given situation, relative to the information values. Figure 7.2 illustrates this idea in showing the possible "mix and match" selection of elements against information values.

Information user grouping is not all-inclusive but shows how the various customers for information security relate to the directives and the levels of protection. Each user set probably has a unique protection requirements mixture.

LEVELS OF DIRECTIVE

A program for electronic information security, for example, uses three levels of directive. The top level is *policy*. A statement of limitations in a very broad sense,

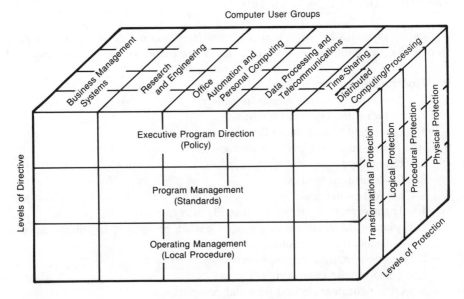

Figure 7.1   Program structure, three-dimensional matrix. (Copyright © James A. Schweitzer, 1980).

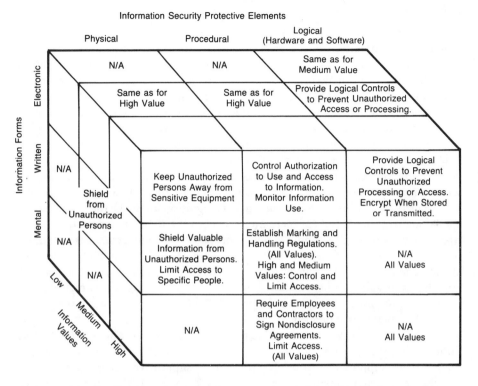

Figure 7.2   Application of security elements across information forms and values.

policy stipulates some desired result with general guidelines on how to achieve the result. A security policy might state that "all company information is private to the company and will be provided sufficient security to guarantee that privacy."

Standards are the second level of directive. A standard establishes an operating mode consistent with and supporting policy. Standards should represent a consensus, among those capable in the particular fields of expertise addressed, on the most desirable way of doing things. Although standards establish common modes of action, they should also leave room for flexibility.

Good standards will allow for flexibility to meet local operating situations, expressed through the lowest level of directive, called *procedure*. Typically, standards are used by systems designers, and procedures are provided at the operating site for systems users. There are many variations on this scenario, which is the beauty of the three-level directive approach. A strong, resilient, practical security system can be built for all situations and circumstances in which information is used.

Policy

Policy is the foundation of the program. Attempts at partial or local protection are not productive for the large business. The term *policy* as used here follows the definition given in *Webster's New Collegiate Dictionary:* "prudence or wisdom in the management of affairs; a definite course or method of action selected from among alternatives and in light of given conditions to guide and determine present and future decisions." Policy is a general guidance from senior management on courses of concern and action. Exactly "how" a thing should be done is left to procedure, a lower level of directive. Policy is so important because it becomes the reference for lower levels of management at distant places and times, when immediate circumstances may require new or unusual courses of action.

Security policy must be based on a recognition that (1) the business has something to protect and (2) there are threats to the things to be protected. The first requirement to developing a policy proposal for management is identification of the "things of value." That is accomplished through the information classification process described. Second, management must understand the general classes of vulnerability sustained by these valuable things (in our case, pieces of information or data). This may be provided through application of the general risk case as previously described.

Each subsequent level of directive refers back to the one above. The "grandfather" directive, the policy, must be crystal clear, and policy must have total management support at top levels. Any partial support or reservations will seriously weaken implementation of the policy throughout the organization, especially if senior line managers have doubts. It may be necessary to go to the top (e.g., the chairman, CEO, operating or managing director) to resolve all the security policy issues, but if so, it is a worthwhile trip.

Characteristics of a Good Policy

A good policy will make clear the following minimum points:

- To whom does it apply?
- When is it effective?
- What is the subject and purpose?
- Who are the key participants (e.g., director of security)?
- How does it work?

A policy for electronic information security should address all aspects of a problem and will be relevant to all appropriate audiences. The policy should

- Provide guidance to all those groups or functions using computers or telecommunications systems (and who may have unique requirements).
- Be constructed to serve as a basis for the development of standards and procedures.

- Address current and near-future technologies, where the most serious exposures are likely.
- Allow flexibility in the light of business requirements.

Many policies fail to include all these characteristics. Some examples of such failures include policies that cover the traditional data processing environment (data center, business systems development function) but do not include time-sharing or personal computing in the research environment. Policy may be written without broadly stated goals being evident, resulting in some people's (the ever-present exceptions to just about anything) being unable or unwilling to visualize the policy's applicability to their case.

Many policies on computer security deal adequately with today's situation but overlook the fact that computing systems technology is developing at a fast pace. A policy written for a static world has little relevance to a business in dynamic change, as most businesses are.

Hard and fast requirements that may be seen by operating management as interference with primary business goals will be bypassed, in one way or another. Therefore, the policy must provide strength and flexibility to allow acknowledgment of critical business goals while retaining assurance of overall protection. Specific needs of user groups are addressed in detailed standards, which in turn are based on the policy.

Management Acceptance of Risk

Any business represents an entrepreneurial risk-taking. To impose a risk-free environment on a business may be an impractical, and certainly very costly, effort. Security policy should therefore allow managers at appropriate levels (depending on the risk involved) to decide to bear risk rather than expend resources on security. As in other weighty business decisions, managers responsible must have the fullest information on the potentials involved.

Essentially the question to be addressed is this: Are the costs of protecting against a given vulnerability so great that, given the worst-case exposure, it is preferable to bear the known risk? (Here is an opportunity to use a limited scope risk analysis.) Notice that this is analogous to many business decisions, where demand, product cost, market share, and so forth are estimated to the best ability. Business is the taking of risks. Security policy must allow management to act responsibly with reasonable flexibility. Acknowledging and choosing to accept risk must be among the established alternatives.

A critical matter in this arrangement is the specification, in policy, of who can make the decision. Generally, a decision to take a risk concerning information at the highest value factor should be reserved for senior corporate executives or division presidents. Decisions concerning information with lesser value factors can be allowed at suitable lower organizational levels.

Developing Corporate Policy

The bedrock on which the program will operate is the corporate policy statement. The policy should be a general statement of goals and intent, based on a survey of the computer security literature and a knowledge of the particular methods and exposures of the business. At minimum, the corporate director of systems, the corporate auditor, and perhaps outside auditors should comprise a steering committee for drafting a policy proposal concerning electronic information processing security. The corporate security manager would serve as recorder and advisor to this group. (The reader is asked to substitute appropriate titles where necessary.) Once a proposed policy is agreed on, it should be circulated among some division systems managers and controllers for comment. This process, or a similar one, will result in a policy statement that is acceptable to all.

The policy should, as far as possible, accommodate future technology applications, at least for the next five years. This is not difficult to do, since the policy is a general statement of intent. For example, a requirement for encryption of highly sensitive data in certain broad circumstances may be currently beyond the ability of the divisions. The policy statement, however, should drive the corporation toward the end posture desired. To do that, the policy must look forward. Remember that there will be an exceptions clause in the policy, as described earlier, so that unavailability of technology can be dealt with in a constructive way.

Exhibit 7.1 illustrates a policy cover letter. The complete policy is found in Appendix 1.

Exhibit 7.1   Policy Cover Letter

XYZ CORPORATION

Office of the Chairman

Subject: Security for digital information

To: Division presidents

The Corporate Review Board has authorized an information security program for XYZ Corporation.

Our increasing use of computers and telecommunications, in all divisions and at all levels of international operations, exposes critical business information to unauthorized observation, theft, modification, or destruction. I am sure you have read of such cases in the business press.

Your interest and support of this program will be necessary. Support in terms of funding and manpower will be required, some on an on-going basis.

I am attaching a copy of the new policy on information security. John Smith, Corporate Security Manager, will be providing you with detailed information on implementation and ongoing management of this important program.

Security Standards: The Program Glue

Security standards are fairly detailed implementing instructions (see Appendix 2) that ensure a level of standardization and compliance with policy across the corporation. The standards should provide sufficient detail on requirements supporting the policy statements so that security coordinators and operating managers can effectively make resource requirements estimations.

The division security coordinators play an important part in developing standards. They may participate in any of several modes, including

- Assigning one of the various sections of the proposed standard to each security coordinator for development, with subsequent review and concurrence by peers.
- Forming a committee of security coordinators for review and approval of standards prepared at corporate level.
- Any combination or similar method to obtain operating unit input.

All divisions should concur with the proposed standards before publication. This may require some tough "horse trading" by the manager of security. Final agreement that the standards meet business requirements is important to later progress in complying with policy. (Table 7.1 shows the areas to be covered by standards.)

One is tempted to issue corporate standards immediately and thus avoid a lengthy, perhaps tedious process. Do not do it—the knowledge of the unit security coordinators about actual operating requirements and problems is a necessary input if good standards are to be developed.

Good standards mean reasonable, practical requirements that *will* be implemented at the unit or division level. Appendix 2 shows a typical set of standards for electronic information security.

Regular meetings of the unit security coordinator with the manager of electronic security are important, especially in the early, formative stages of the program. In larger companies, some sort of regular newsletter or memo from the security manager is recommended. This newsletter can be very informal but should contain technology developments, top management outlooks on security, and information on the planned meetings and subjects and should also serve as a cross-fertilization medium. The unit or division security coordinators are both the developmental mechanism for the program and the means for ensuring its strength and capabilities. The network of security coordinators may be viewed as the skeleton of the program; the standards and unit procedures are the muscle. Without the framework of the security coordinators, constantly developing and implementing technology application changes, the program will become redundant. Once electronic security standards have been agreed on and published, the security coordinators should be asked to do a detailed survey. This we will call a requirements survey. The operating divisions or units can now make fairly

Table 7.1   Electronic Information Security Standards by Subject Areas

---

General
  Information valuation
  Information protection: marking and handling
  Logical access management
  Levels of protection
  Security elements
  Program management responsibilities

Data processing and telecommunications operation
  Input and output processing
  Facilities access controls
  Management controls over operating environment
  User services
  Administration

Business systems development
  Security requirements in phased development process
    Design
    Programming
    Installation
    Review

Office systems
  Professional workstations
  Word processing
  Distributed office systems
  Facsimile and reprographics systems

Engineering and research systems
  Personal terminals
  Minicomputers
  Laboratory computing

---

specific estimates of resources and costs, since they have the published security standards as a yardstick.

Procedures

Procedures are local instructions that adapt standards requirements to local needs, which may be unique to an individual data center, office, or plant. These decisions are not readily made at a management level. Therefore, we do not discuss procedures development in detail here.

LEVELS OF PROTECTION

Every security system contains multiple levels of protection. Even on the personal level, the individual's security system has several levels. Depending on the individual, these levels may be (1) avoid trouble, (2) run away, (3) fight back, and (4) accept attack while minimizing bodily harm.

Various levels of protection may be implicit in many security systems, but for the purposes of electronic information security, the levels should be expressed explicitly. These levels are shown in Figure 7.3 as a series of concentric circles. Conceptually, penetration through each succeeding level inward should be increasingly difficult. In practice, one or more levels may be bypassed by a penetrator, as we shall see.

The right-end plane of the three-dimensional matrix in Figure 7.1 shows the security elements required for the protection of information as occurring in four levels. The levels are related to the characteristics and placement of the security elements. Physical, procedural, and logical protection levels are always required

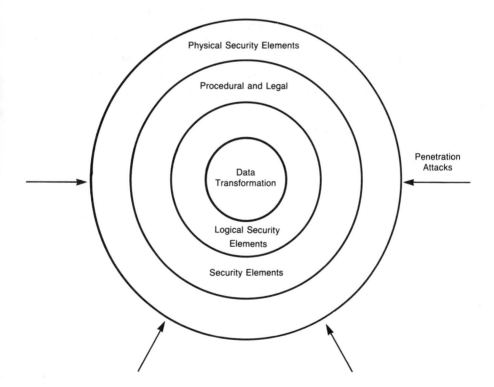

Figure 7.3   Concentric levels of protection.

for any information having an established value factor. Transformational protection is required only in special cases of a high-value factor.

Physical Protection (Level 1)

Physical security, or the separation of physical assets from potential harm, is a basic need for any kind of security program, and it is the underpinning for an information security program. Level 1 refers to all those security elements necessary to ensure that unauthorized persons are excluded from physical spaces and assets where their presence represents a potential threat. All types of computers, computing devices, and associated communications facilities must be considered as sensitive assets and spaces and be protected accordingly.

Physical security elements include, but are not limited to, the following:

1. Physical access controls, including guards and receptionists, door access controls (keys, magnetic cards, digital code keypads, voice recognition, hand recognition, employee badge examination), restricted areas (special authorization required), perimeter lighting and fencing, high-strength glass, closed-circuit television monitors, automatic door controls, and human traps.
2. Locks and special protective features on cabinets, closets, and compartments for protecting magnetic media (tapes, disks, cartridges) and reports containing information with established value factors. Vault-type doors for media libraries, laboratories, and other sensitive areas also fall into this category of physical elements.

Procedural Protection (Level 2)

Procedural and legal security elements consist of those arrangements of employee interfaces that will ensure integrity and security of assets. Organizational and procedural elements include the following:

1. Authorization to use. The information owner, the person primarily responsible for the functional area in which the information originates, is budgeted for, or which is assigned control, must decide whom to authorize to see, modify, or remove information. These authorities may be implemented through logical access control systems or by procedures. The general rationale is that a person must have a business-related "need to know."
2. Organizational compartmentalization to provide a series of checks and balances. For example, the electronic data processing auditors should not report to the senior data processing executive but rather to the corporate treasurer or some other disinterested senior fiscal officer. This will help objective reporting of exposures. In a data center, data control (which validates outputs)

should be separate organizationally from the computer operations producing those outputs.

3. Procedural assignments that will provide a check on integrity and security. For example, computer tapes being selected for a process by the tape librarian are also checked, before operation, by a quality assurance function. After the production run, output tapes are checked by data control and by the librarian. (The obvious analogy is the cashier and the daily cash count by a second party.)

4. Legal protection. Mental information is protected by having the person knowing the information sign a confidentiality agreement. Chapter 6 discusses this in some detail.

Logical Protection (Level 3)

Logical security elements consist of those hardware and software features provided in a system that helps to ensure the integrity and security of data, programs, and operating systems (for which the references offer details). Such logical elements may include the following:

1. Hardware elements that segregate core and thus present overlap, accidental or intentional; core clearing after a job to prevent the following job seizing control; levels of privileges that restrict access to the operating system programs; hard-wired (firmware) programs that are not software-modifiable, and similar elements.

2. Software elements that provide access management capabilities. These are the key security elements in a program to protect electronic information. An effective logical security system provides the means to identify, authenticate, authorize, or limit the authenticated user to certain previously stipulated actions, for each system user who may "sign on" or for each program that may be called on by the computer to process files with established value factors. (See Appendix 3, Automated Logical Access Control.)

Passwords are the most commonly used method for controlling access to computers and information serviced thereon. A password is similar to an unlisted telephone number. Some people know the number (e.g., the telephone company employees) because they must process it; other people are given the number by the principal (owner of the telephone). Both cases can negate the privacy value of the unlisted number by exposing it or by allowing use of it in ways the principal will not like.

Most passwords are merely words or numbers selected by the user of the computer. In some cases the computer itself provides the password. In either instance, the password is usually private to an individual. If the user divulges the password to others, or exposes it so that other people know it, the password's efficacy as a security element is compromised or destroyed.

The most serious weakness of passwords relates to a common human failing, forgetfulness. People write the passwords on their desk blotters, in telephone list finders, on the walls, or even on the terminals so that they will not have to depend on memory.

The majority of passwords in use have characteristics of personal significance to the user. This means that the passwords are easy to deduce, especially for someone with training. Given names, children's names, birth or wedding dates, and home addresses are all very popular, because most users remember those things readily.

In today's systems, a single password is often the only security element between the would-be penetrator (an unauthorized user) and an entire array of data files and processes. This is similar to the lock on the typical house—once a penetrator is inside, all the contents are available. In computing, this is an extremely hazardous arrangement. Many of the vulnerabilities associated with passwords result from one or more of a set of common failings, as follows.

Passwords are improperly constructed, in that they are obvious or easily deduced or have so few characters as to be subject to statistical attack (i.e., there are too few possibilities).

Passwords are never, or very seldom, changed. Even if a password owner takes "reasonable" care of the password, over time it will become known to others. This may occur because of careless talk, observation of password key-in, failure to protect security listings of passwords, or accidental or intentional penetration to password files.

Passwords are not kept private. Often, password owners share access with others because of business requirements, camaraderie, or carelessness. Although sharing may be only mildly vulnerable, unless the password is promptly changed one can assume that the password will quickly become general knowledge throughout the department or area.

Access management is the generic name for the set of security elements developed and applied for the purpose of controlling access to information. An effective access management system has three parts or functions, as follows:

1. Identification. A claim to be a certain person—an individual wishing to access information on a computer enters an *identification* code.
2. Authentication. A proof of the claimed identity—the individual offers something inherent (voice print, for example), something known (password), or something possessed (a plastic magnetically encoded card) as *authentication* of the claimed identity.
3. Authorization. The computer or communications system determines the allowable actions for that individual. A preset table or list is referred to, providing *authorization* for the individual to see, move, change, or operate on information in certain files or with certain characteristics. Any or all functions may be authorized by the "information owner."

Passwords are traditionally used for the identification and authentication steps in the access management process. A typical sequence would be

SIGN ON
ACCOUNT NUMBER: 12345A (identification)
PASSWORD: J. ARNOLD (authentication)
SELECT FUNCTION: READ
SELECT FILE: ABACUS 3 (authorization)
ABACUS 3 NOT VALID. TRY ANOTHER (attempt rejected, not authorized)

In this typical case, the account number is really not a security construct because it is probably publicly known (within the organization of the password owner). The password itself is very weak, since it is probably a name related directly to the password owner. It will be deduced easily.

If the computer system does not automatically require password changes, the password "J. ARNOLD" has probably not been changed for years. In such a case we must assume that both the account number and the password in the example are known and are hence worthless as security elements. In fact, they are dangerous, because they give the impression of security but offer none against someone familiar with the system and intentionally trying to penetrate.

Improving Access Management

Passwords can be strengthened by improving the quality of the passwords themselves and by combining passwords with supporting security elements. A password system of high quality has the following characteristics:

1. The password has at least eight characters in it. Mathematically, a password of seven or more characters offers great resistance to statistical attack. (We have to assume that an attempted penetration has computing support.)
2. The password is randomly constructed and has no relationship to the owner's environment. It contains nothing relatable to the owner's person, family, or company job. (It could be computer-generated.) It is not a dictionary word.
3. The password is protected in a manner consonant with the value factor of the information being protected.
4. The password is changed regularly. In most cases, the password should be changed at least once every three months. (In one actual case, persons having obtained passwords illicitly were able to use them six months later, to steal computer services.)

For an excellent explanation of the effect of password construction on security, see *Modern Methods for Computer Security and Privacy,* by Lance Hoffman.[20]

People in the business environment are unlikely to be motivated to ensure effective passwording. People just do not want to be bothered. Some complementary measures that strengthen password effectiveness are as follows:

1. Program the security software system to force password changes and automatically cut off people attempting trial-and-error access after *x* number of tries.
2. Provide administrative tracking of password changes, based on printouts from the computer system showing dates when last password change occurred. The security coordinator can then follow up to remind computer users to change passwords.
3. Store all passwords in encrypted computer files. Passwords transmitted over communications circuits should always be in encrypted form.
4. Printing or display should always be suppressed when passwords are entered to a terminal keyboard.
5. A transform can be used as a "handshaking" procedure. In this method, the user has established a formula, such as $X = 3A + 10$. The computer would offer a value for A; the user, being the only person knowing the formula, would respond with a value for X.

Biometrics

Biometrics refers to the science of using physical characteristics for authentication. In the triage of "what you know (password), what you have (magnetic card or smart card), and what you are (fingerprint)," biometrics addresses the last. Using a bodily physical characteristic for authentication provides a reliable and robust proof of identity. Current systems for identifying a person use the pattern in the retina of the eye, or fingerprints, or hand geometry. Voiceprints and signature analysis systems are in limited use but may not yet be as reliable as the other three methods.

The costs of using such a system relate to the cost of technology (unacceptably high at present for most general business applications) and the cost of possible false acceptances or false rejections. These result when the system is set to a very fine tolerance (e.g., an authorized person with a slightly swollen hand may be rejected) or to a coarse tolerance (e.g., an unauthorized person may be allowed access.

As experience with these biometrics-based authentication systems builds, and as better security is demanded, we will see a gradual conversion, in critical security applications, from the relatively weak password systems to methods that combine elements from the "have, know, are" authentication sets. Biometrics, because of their intrinsic reliability (how often can one cut off a person's finger to do an impersonation?), are sure to be essential parts of these new authentication systems.

Probably the most important factor in an effective authentication scheme is the will of the users to make it work.

Transformational Protection (Encryption)

Encryption is the use of the ancient science of cryptography (literally, "secret writing") for information processing security requirements (in the sense used here, "information processing" includes computer application systems, telecommunications and data networking, computer terminals and communicating office equipment, and the use of all types of magnetic storage media). Cryptography has been a military art throughout most of recorded history. More recently, a science of cryptography has developed as a result of demands from the community of computer users.

Encryption is accomplished through the coding-decoding of information by using mathematical formulas (algorithms) and secret or public keys. A myraid of methods exists for performing encryption, based on various mathematical principles and properties. The system chosen should

- Protect in the environment used (e.g., against the level of threat)
- Provide protection at a cost acceptable to the user (typically, processing overhead)
- Not interfere with business operations

Table 7.2 provides a glossary of encryption terminology.

In practice, data encryption is achieved through the use of an appropriate algorithm and a key. The algorithm is a set of rules or steps for performing a specified operation (encoding). The algorithm may be processed by a program-

Table 7.2   A Glossary of Encryption Terms

Algorithm: A set of rules for performing a task.
Cipher: A form of cryptography employing a transformation of the information itself, based on a key, as the means of concealment.
Ciphertext: The results of enciphering plaintext.
Cryptography: The science of secret writing.
Decipher: To transform, using a key, from ciphertext back into plaintext.
Decrypt: To transform unintelligible information into intelligible information.
Encipher: To transform, using a key, from plaintext to ciphertext.
Encrypt: To render information unintelligible using a transformation algorithm.
Key: The secret controlling variable of an encryption algorithm specifying a particular transformation.
Plaintext: A readable message or data before encryption or after decryption.

mable piece of computer equipment, or a set of electronic circuits can be constructed to perform the computations (hardware-implemented software).

The key is the "secret" part of the encryption system. Having a key enables a person or computer to encrypt or decrypt messages (data streams). Everyone may know what the algorithm (formula) is, but only those so authorized should have the key. Since there typically are hundreds of billions (2^{56}) of keys available for a reliable encryption algorithm, there is little fear that someone may guess or chance on the key.

The key is typically a very large number (ten to twenty digits long). The keys may be computer generated as random numbers. The confidentiality of the sensitive data may depend on the protection given to the key. For example, network control devices (minicomputers) may be used to create and distribute keys as required without any human knowledge of the keys. In the "public key" system, one part of the key may be publicly known, as are telephone numbers, associated with the "owner's" name. See below for a description of this system.

In the past twenty years, government and business have recognized the hazards in the growing traffic of information on and among computers and computer devices. For the first time, nonmilitary applications for encryption technology have been recognized. The U.S. Department of Commerce, through the Institute for Computer Sciences and Technology at the National Institute for Standards and Technology, initiated an effort to provide a standard for data protection during transmission or while in storage. In conjunction with IBM Corporation, the data encryption standard (DES) was developed. This algorithm has been adopted as the standard for unclassified information being transmitted or stored electronically. Sensitive business information managers may use the DES algorithm without hesitation, since the strength of the standard lies in the keys being used. As a result, techniques and devices are now being commercially developed to implement computer-based encryption systems.

The algorithm used in an encryption system need not be kept secret if well designed. An important part of an effective encryption security method is that everyone knows how it works and recognizes the difficulties in breaking its code. The cipher key of course must be kept secret. The key should be classified at the same level as the data it protects. Although truly unbreakable systems can be devised using one-time keys of a length greater than the text, this is impractical in the business situation. Today's encryption systems, in use in commercial applications, use fixed-length, relatively short keys, which are used many times except where key generation is automated.

The systems assume that a would-be penetrator has plaintext and ciphertext of the same message with which to determine the key. The strength of an effective cryptosystem lies in the probability of such success, which is so small as to require enormous computer resources to make an attempt with reasonable hope of penetration. The system, then, can always be broken given sufficient effort; the defense lies in the time, effort, and resources the penetrator must expend to break the code. This "work factor" applies to all security mechanisms. That is, no security system is impenetrable but is considered sufficient if an attacker must use resources whose cost is unacceptable in light of anticipated gain.

The algorithm used to encipher information is considered acceptably strong, in terms of the work factor it provides, if

1. The mathematical equations describing the algorithm's operation are so complex that, for all practical purposes, it is not possible to solve for the key using analytical methods.
2. It is too costly to employ methods that are mathematically less complicated because too much time is required, as in the case of key exhaustion, or too much data storage is required, as in the case of certain statistical attacks.[21]

As in the design of any defensive mechanism, assumptions are made concerning the attacker's capabilities and resources:

1. Relatively large amounts of plaintext (specified by the analyst, if so desired) and corresponding ciphertext are available.
2. All details of the algorithm are available. (It is assumed that cryptographic strength must not depend on a requirement to maintain the secrecy of the cryptographic algorithm.)
3. A number of large high-speed computers (determined by the resources available to the opponent) can be used for cryptanalysis.

In the case of computer-processed information, the work factor may be considered sufficiently rigorous if solution of the key identity is computationally infeasible; that is, if it would require an inordinate resource or time, or if the method for doing the problem is unknown to the mathematical community.

Many different methods may be used to implement an encryption method. In computer information processing, stream ciphers and block ciphers are used, primarily because these methods lend themselves well to binary notation and the operating characteristics of computer systems and, more important, because they provide great strength of security.

Using Encryption

Attacks against business information in computer-based systems fall into three categories.

1. Wiretapping, or the collection of information through physical connection or radiation evaluation. The penetrator records a bit stream and then may analyze the data more or less at leisure.
2. Terminal penetration, where the attacker uses inherent system weakness to discover passwords or to manipulate the operating system or the security

system itself. The penetrator can see or destroy files, plant time-driven programs to do various clandestine tasks, or create self-destruction schemes affecting hardware reliability, software accuracy, and data output integrity.

3. Physical theft of information on magnetic media, through actual removal from company premises, or by surreptitious copying and removal of the copied media.

In the categories described, the use of encryption increases the penetration work factor (cost to penetrate) enormously.

Achieving Protection

Although wiretapping generally cannot be prevented, some types of attack can be reliably detected through good communications protocols. These attacks include message stream modification, denial of services, and spurious connection. Other wiretapping, which includes observation of message information and analysis of traffic patterns, cannot be detected, but damage may be limited through proper use of encryption. In all cases, attainment of security goals is based on the difficulty the penetrator faces in attempting to defeat the encryption algorithm.[22]

Terminal-originating penetration attempts result from weakness in the operating system, failure to administer the security subsystem, employee error and laxity, and incomplete or ineffective access management systems. There is no way to guarantee that penetration will not take place. The encryption of high-value-factor business files ensures that the penetrator who can cut through the security subsystem to access on-line information files will get only gibberish for his or her trouble. (Data in work spaces of a computer are always cleartext, and a penetrator into such work space is not affected by encryption.)

Surreptitious removal of correspondence or data files stored on magnetic media is essentially a matter of good physical security and office discipline. Proper media control requires item numbering, inventory records, careful placement, and active management. Despite these security elements, people do and will remove magnetic media from business premises for varying purposes, some of which may be illegitimate. (This vulnerability will become increasingly severe as the "advanced electronic office" develops; it is already serious in data centers.) If the information on the media (tapes, disks, etc.) is encrypted, the unauthorized possessor will not be able to decipher the data contents.

A clear, readily demonstrated rule on the alternatives of implementation of encryption, in terms of hardware versus software, is impossible at this time. This is so because so many cryptosystems are being developed, and because all of the developments are in the early stages (first-generation products).

Generally, requirements should dictate the implementation method used. If relatively small amounts of data are to be encrypted for use by a small group of people, such as a timesharing system with some sensitive files, a software implementation is probably the best. Original cost (for a commercial package) will be reasonable, and use will seldom be enough to avoid running up big overhead processing charges.

If large streams of data are to be processed, especially where a link or heavily used data path is involved, hardware is superior to software. Encryption hardware manufacturers are developing increasingly efficient, miniaturized products. Operating costs consist of a small overhead and the administration of keys (no small matter in a big network).

Hardware, at this stage, must be considered more secure than software, since there is reduced potential for already present or induced software "bugs"; that is, the hardware cannot be modified easily. Also, software computation in support of either method is much more expensive than hardware implementation, and in some cases overhead can approach 100%.

Software-implemented encryption packages (encryption through the processing of a program of instructions) are commercially available. Some require typical key administration. Others (e.g., Raviv transform) use the statistical characteristics of the data to be encrypted, with a random number generator, to create internal keys. Since these keys are recreated whenever the particular data set is encrypted or decrypted, there is little or no key management effort involved. The keys are processed under protection of the encryption system, in encrypted form. Certain of these software packages generate keys with lengths equal to the data itself. As mentioned above, this is the most secure situation from the point of potential breaking of the cryptosystem.

The software encryption system is maintained on the computer program library along with other application programs. The encryption program is "called" and operates against the file to be encrypted or decrypted. The exact mode of activity is determined by the data set condition when the software encounters it; that is, if data are encrypted, it is decryption mode, and vice versa.

As is true with most security systems, encryption requires an administrative effort. If encryption is to provide real protection, a significant administrative effort is necessary to manage the control and distribution of the encryption keys. In a network security system, key administration can be automated, thus eliminating most manual effort but creating a systems cost.

Usually, two levels of keys are used; the terminology applied to the levels depends on the system or author describing the method. For a basic understanding, the keys may be regarded as the primary and secondary keys.

- Primary key: The primary key (PK) is distributed by messenger or registered mail for entry to the encryption device or program. Its purpose is to authenticate secondary keys, thus avoiding the requirement to use a messenger or registered mail when a secondary key is to be changed. Each node or receive-send location may have a unique PK.
- Secondary key: The secondary key (SK) may be changed as desired. The SK may be used for only one session or for discrete data flow. The SK may be changed every day, week, month, or otherwise periodically. In some cases, the SK may be used for only one message, then discarded. This is a high-

security method typical to the military and intelligence communities. When the SK is changed, it is encrypted with the primary key and transmitted as data to the receiving device or software. Since various nodes may have unique primary keys, even an interception or misrouting of a new SK would not compromise security.

The network security manager (or the automated network system controller) must maintain a safe file for storage of keys and must keep records of the keys used for various links, sessions, or locations. If an encryption key is confused or lost, the data are not recoverable. Therefore, efficient means must be established for key recordkeeping and protection.

Some manufacturers provide hand-held devices for loading the primary key. The device may be stored at each location in a safe. It then may be used to reload the primary key should a power or equipment failure require it. It is impossible to read out the primary key from the device, since it will generate only into a specified encryption module and uses light emissions as a carrier. Tampering with the sealed device immediately destroys the key.

The key management process is somewhat different for each system, but a general procedure may be described as follows (an automated process follows a similar sequence):

1. After installation of the proper hardware or software, the responsible security manager (SM) generates one or more primary keys. The system will usually provide random number generator means for developing secure keys. Once the key is developed, it is read out, either into a portable loading device, as described above, or as a long series of digits which are hand copied and protected.

2. The SM makes a copy of the primary key and places it in his or her safe with the necessary descriptive indications (where to be used, etc.). Complete records are necessary. The SM then delivers the primary key(s) to the locations required. These locations could be the ends of a communications link, nodes in a network, specific user offices, etc. Distribution of the keys, as high-value-factor information, is done by messenger or by registered mail.

3. At the receiving locations, the primary key is loaded into the equipment or software, by keying-in or by use of the hardware device described above. Documents describing the primary keys are then destroyed, locked in a safe, or returned to the SM, depending on the system chosen. For best security, only the SM should have a copy of the primary keys. (This is not true when a hardware loading device is in use. The device is always kept in a safe, however.)

4. Once primary keys are loaded, the SM may generate secondary keys, which are then sent to the proper locations as encrypted messages (encrypted with the primary key). If an acknowledgment is received from the receiving locations, the primary keys are successfully loaded and the system is ready to operate.

5. Routine encryption may commence using the secondary key to encrypt the protected data. Secondary keys may be changed as desired, using the primary key facility. More frequent changes of secondary keys increase cost and improve the security protection.

A manual procedure is described to illustrate the process. In practice, key generation, distribution, and management will probably be done by automated means.

Public Key Encryption

A clever process, using the characteristics of very large prime numbers, allows encryption using a "public key" system. Actually, the system, developed at MIT (Rivest et al. 1977),[23] provides each user with both a public key and a private key. Since there is today no convenient way, short of harnessing very large computers in multiple formations, to determine the factors of a product of two large prime numbers, the public key system provides excellent protection and convenience, avoiding the usual key management issues. The public key method, in simple concept, allows user *A* to encrypt a message using *A*'s secret key and *B*'s public key (which may be published in a directory). Upon receipt, *B* decrypts the message using *A*'s public key and *B*'s private key. The results not only deliver the message but can prove that *A* is in fact the originator.

The public key process is commercially available and was chosen in early 1989 as the basis for securing message traffic on the Internet, the collection of networks sponsored by governmental and educational institutions in the United States. Simultaneously, Digital Equipment Corporation chose the public key system for a means of authenticating message traffic on networks. Thus, it appears that the public key system (known commercially as the RSA system) will become the primary method for securing information on networks.[23]

The Penetration Work Factor

The basic concept for spending money on information security is that one assumes that a miscreant will not have unlimited time or resources to attempt information destruction, observation, or modification. The same reasoning applies to home security. We put in reasonably good locks but assume that the burglar will not appear at the house with a bulldozer or chain saw or erect a tent to spend days working at the door.

The penetration work factor (PWF) refers to the effort that someone must expend to do intended mischief. Security is established with the goal of extending the PWF to the point at which the perceived value of the target (information or mischief) is less than the perceived value of the penetration effort. Hence, for a middle-value file, we want to make the perpetrator put forth some extended effort, either in breaking and entering, in paying off dishonest employees, or in running computer processes. At some point, we hope, the person decides he or she can find easier pickings, and moves on. Of course, any determined penetrator with unlimited resources (the CIA?) will eventually break through. For high-value information, the appropriate work factor is always established through encryption, the ultimate security method.

Each level of protection in the three-dimensional matrix (see Fig. 7.1) contains a set of security elements, or features. These security elements are cumulative in the sense that they increase the PWF, or the effort required of a penetrator. The PWF, or total effort required along with risk of discovery, will contribute to decisions by the penetrator on method, time to be expended, value of results, liability if caught, and so forth. The PWF is a deterrent. A strong PWF, evident to the penetrator, means that the stakes must be high for continued penetration effort (see Fig. 8.2).

The PWF itself may indicate that, at best, only partial information will be obtained. A discouraged penetrator is a thwarted penetrator. Before discussing some cases where the PWF was ineffective, we can postulate some rules about security elements.

1. Electronic information security measures should be publicized. Their resistance to attack must be depend on the measures themselves being secret. For example, a password access control depends on a password construction of sufficient strength, plus frequent changes of passwords. The passwords themselves are secret. The procedure for providing and changing passwords should be publicized as a part of systems installation processes.
2. Sufficient security elements must be provided in each concentric level to ensure that all avenues of penetration are covered. At the logical level, for example, access management control must be established over operating system software maintenance activities. There is little to be gained in closing doors through identification and authentication measures controlling terminal access if internal systems doors are unguarded.

Figure 7.4 illustrates the security elements. Keep in mind that an exhaustive list is impossible. Novel situations almost always result in new measures, which may represent elements not previously recognized.

The requirements for applicability and importance of the levels of protection and their security elements are best seen through the use of case examples. For each case, which has been developed from real-life situations, an analysis is provided. Keep in mind that there is no finite list of security elements. Those indicated in the analysis as being causal may have been incomplete in themselves or improperly applied.

Case 1

Janice Smith was a sterling employee, intelligent, well motivated, and a whiz at programming. The data processing manager was disappointed when Janice resigned. A gala farewell party was held. Janice, however, did not feel as sorrowful

Level 1 (Outer)	Physical Security
Perimeter control: Building control: Area control:	fencing, lighting, access controls access control, visitor restrictions, badges inside restricted areas, access restrictions
Level 2	Organizational and Procedural Security
Organizational Security:	definition and separation of duties, shared responsibility
Procedural Security:	fiscal controls written procedure supervision work review process control materials control document marking
Level 3	Logical Security
Hardware Security:	functional separation of processes, read-only memory, core clearing
Software Security:	privileged instructions, access control subsystems, access management packages, security kernel
Level 4 (Innermost)	Data Transformation

Encryption systems
    hardware:
 	
    software:
	
	communications link
	communications network
	write-to-media (channel control)
	write-to-media
	pretransmission
	callable programs

PENETRATION

Figure 7.4   Security levels and elements.

at the parting as some others. She rented a terminal and set up a consulting business from her apartment, using her ex-employer's computer. Business was good. Janice became greedy and decided to store her customer's files on the computer, in addition to the programming that she had been doing. After a few months, the excessive use of disk file space became evident to the computer's owners. Janice's files were erased, and her password was eliminated from the authorization file.

Analysis:

Levels of Protection	Status at Time of Incident	Causal Situation
Physical	In place	Not relevant
Organizational-procedural	Weak	Failure to change authorization
Logical	In place	Ineffective due to procedural failure
Data transformation	Not used	

Case 2

ABC company used an on-line process control system. Modifications were continually being made because of product mix changes and varying characteristics of raw materials. Programmers made changes to the system programs by means of password-authenticated entry to the program library. Chris Allen was discharged by the programming manager at ABC because of poor attitude and job performance deficiencies. The following day, ABC programmers discovered they could no longer access the program libraries, the password file having been changed by persons unknown. An investigation showed that Chris Allen had been allowed to return to the programming work area for a time before leaving the ABC facility. System records showed the passwords had been changed from his terminal.

Analysis:

Levels of Protection	Status at Time of Incident	Causal Situation
Physical	In place	Not relevant
Organizational-procedural	Poor discharge procedure	Should have been escorted from facility
Logical	Poor security for password file	Should not have been able to change other than own password
Data transformation	Not used	

Case 3

Employees of a racetrack were able to modify programs on a backup computer and thereby generate winning tickets after a race was completed but before the wagering results were computed. They in effect stole from the winners by adding more winning tickets to the number, splitting the winner's pool.

Analysis:

Levels of Protection	Status at Time of Incident	Causal Situation
Physical	In place	Not relevant
Organizational-procedural	Poor supervision, poor procedure	Employees able to violate system procedure repeatedly
Logical	Weak security for operating system	Operators able to change data files and access privileged programs
Data transformation	Not used	

Case 4

A stockbroker planned to make a profit by obtaining information on strategic buying from a large competitor's files. He was able to identify a telephone line used for transaction data traffic. By climbing a pole, he tapped the line and copied off all the data traffic. Using a small computer, he was able to analyze the traffic and obtain information on volume buy orders before they were completed.

Analysis:

Levels of Protection	Status at Time of Incident	Causal Situation
Physical	In place	Bypassed
Organizational-procedural	In place	Not relevant
Logical	Not applicable	
Data transformation	Not used	Encryption would have denied information to penetrator

These cases illustrate the common failings in security programs:

1. Security elements provided do not cover all the exposures. Some security elements are in place in every case; nevertheless, penetrators succeeded.
2. Security elements are not properly maintained or administered. Even though passwords or other access control methods are used, failure to change them at appropriate times or to use effective forms negates their value as protective measures.

No security program, including the one proposed in this book, can provide perfect security. But many businesses may have security coverage that is in fact a placebo. The business managers feel secure but are not. This is a very dangerous situation, worse than the case where the business has no security and is nervously accepting acknowledged risk.

A program for information security must include security elements in all four levels of protection. The security elements must reasonably cover all the vulnerabilities, must be rigorous and offer resistance against attack, must pose a significant work factor to the penetrator, and must always be in effect.

Specific details on a suggested standard are provided in Appendix 2. A selection of valuable options in security elements for the four levels of protection can be found in the References at the end of the book.

INFORMATION USER GROUPS

The computer user groups in the top plane of the matrix (Figure 7.1) represent a convenience grouping that may vary according to the style and organization of a business. For example, in some businesses, information processing activities supporting business management functions (e.g., accounting, customer services) are highly structured, while scientific information processing is largely free form. Security rules and practices for one group may be confusing to another, because terminology is different. Office workers, for another example, have environments different from those of production or engineering workers, although both may use terminals and automated office-type equipment. (Eventually, security will depend on individual motivation!)

The user groups, then, are a recognition of the need to provide security requirements tailored to the work situation. The reader should anticipate a need to define user groups according to the practices and organization of the particular business.

People using computing in the various parts of a business view the computer differently. The view of one person may be completely different from that of another. Hence, the computer security rules may be more effective if provided in a context harmonious with the viewpoint of the computer user audiences.

Consider a secretary, a scientist, and a programmer working on business systems. All three may use computers extensively. The secretary has an advanced office processor that does word processing and communications and can retrieve data from a central file. The scientist has a terminal, almost exclusively used for mathematical processes, with a small printer. The business programmer is working at a terminal in a highly structured environment, developing programs that are part of a large system.

Each of these people is using a computer, but the working environment, vocabulary, and understanding of the basic technology applied differ widely. Preparing a security procedure to fit each group is more effective and "friendlier" than attempting to use a generalization. In the reader's business situation, the groups or their characteristics may vary from those discussed here, but the concept remains.

Business Management Systems

Business management systems consist, for our purposes, of those applications (computer hardware, communications systems, and software) supporting the general processes of business. These processes include accounts payable and accounts receivable systems, inventory control systems, payroll and treasury systems, and customer and employee recordkeeping systems. Such systems are typically "batch processing." (For example, a payroll system where time tickets are processed or key-entered in batches, updating files and generating a "batch" of outputs, in one cyclical run.)

Separation of business systems from other types of computer applications is done to make description of security processes simpler. Many of the various types of systems may interface and exchange data; some may be closely coupled.

Segregation of business, research, office, and communications systems is done because experience has shown that the "audience groups" using these systems require different security approaches. Where business systems offer remote access to files through terminals, security is covered below.

From an electronic information security viewpoint, business systems may be considered to have five parts, related to the traditional systems life cycle:

1. Business systems analysis and programming
2. Input processing
3. Data processing operations
4. Output processing
5. Maintenance

Security in the Business Systems Development Process

Systems analysis and programming are key activities in the information security process. Security elements (as previously described) must be "built-in" to the business systems during the design process. From a management outlook, good control of business system development is closely related to good security. In other words, the use of a rigorous phased systems development process is critical both to investment control and to security.

In certain phases of development, where management review is provided, auditors or other reviewers representing management must ascertain that suitable security elements are included in the design and programming of the system. Table 7.3 illustrates phases and related security efforts.

The first of these security reviews must be at an early phase of system development. At minimum, a phase I or phase II review should establish that an information value factor for the data to be processed has been determined and

Table 7.3   Phased Development and Security

Phase	Activity	Related Information Security Work
I	Requirements definition	Determine business sensitivity and degree of security required.
II	System specification	Establish data value factors. Determine security specifications.
III	System engineering	Develop manual-logical access control procedure.
IV	Test and installation	Security review and audit preinstallation Postinstallation security test
V	Maintenance	Audit System efficiency testing

that suitable (according to policy and standards) security measures are planned and described in the system specifications. The ability of the systems analysts and programmers to provide security mechanisms depends on the existence of adequate standards based on policy, as discussed earlier. The information security standards are then the basis for phase reviews of the security elements being built into the system.

Later phase reviews, at those phases addressing final testing and data center acceptance, must address the testing of the efficacy of the security elements in the real-life use of the system, both in terms of information processing and in the input/output activities closely related to process design.

Business systems documentation must include thorough instructions for the users and processors of system data concerning the electronic security measures required. The documentation should spell out, among other things, how access authorizations are granted and effected (e.g., how does a prospective user obtain approval to access data, and how does one get a password?); who controls such authorizations; marking and control requirements for outputs, both hard and soft (CRT) copy (generally directly related to established value factor); and last, tape or other media retention and protection requirements.

The business systems development process itself requires a significant level of security. Systems design documents, programming worksheets, program listing, and overall systems documentation should be provided security commensurate with the value factor assigned to the data to be processed. In other words, the systems documentation and program listings should be assigned value factor equal to that assigned to the system's information. This means that access to systems design and programming areas, on-line terminals, on-line files, documentation libraries, working papers, and so on must be restricted to those employees needing to know based on job assignment.

Business applications programming is a severe security risk in business today. In most companies, programmers operate in a "club" atmosphere, surrounded by mystery. One need only read any of the available books on programmer productivity to realize that programmers, by and large, are not managed today. Many will have carte blanche access to any systems or information, often through on-line terminals ostensibly provided for program maintenance and development. These terminals may also be used for secret programming to accomplish unauthorized ends. Good business practice and minimal security and data integrity require that all business programming be done in a controlled environment. Such an environment includes

- All testing and maintenance done through a "base case" or duplicate of the actual business files.
- All program maintenance changes approved by three levels of management:
  1. Management of using function
  2. Programming management
  3. Data center management
- All programmer access to a computer is through password-verified authentication mechanisms. (It is interesting to note that, contrary to initial reaction, controlled programming environments are well liked by managers once properly implemented. Good control is good management.)

Without these minimal control measures, management is literally turning business control over to the journeyman programmers.

An illustration of an information security standard for business data processing is shown in Appendix 2.

Research and Engineering

Consider the researcher who is using a personal minicomputer to perform studies bearing on a new product. A breakthrough occurs—does the employee instinctively act to protect this information? Does he or she know how to mark, cover, store, and disseminate information with a high-value factor? Remember, this may be novel information. No precedent exists for its value. The researcher may run down the hallways shouting to the world, "Eureka, I've found it!" and tell everyone who will listen. Or he or she may create a file and send it (electronically?) to impress other people, with no consideration for security. If the researcher is security conscious and properly motivated, however, the information will be stored in a password-protected file. The password will be a new one, strong enough to resist attack. Any reports produced will be marked and wrapped for delivery according to established information protection procedures. If the information is transmitted in electronic form to others in the research community (very likely in an automated research and development environment), it will be encrypted to ensure security or privacy. Similar scenarios can be imagined for offices, plants, and other business environments. The existence of the mechanics of a program for security, in themselves, just cannot do the job in the computer age. Employee motivation is the key to achieving information security, and the unit or division security coordinator is the prime mover in this effort.

Effective security for information processed or stored in the research and engineering environment requires carefully developed, well-enunciated standards. Such standards must recognize and emphasize the personal responsibilities of each computer user for the recognition and protection of information. Where appropriate, each user should have precise instructions on recognizing information values, which should result in the employee's providing protection to the information, whether in digital or human-readable form, commensurate with its value.

General rules concerning data centers and traditional applications processing do not apply here. One person may serve as system designer, programmer, operator, tape-disk librarian, output clerk, and ultimate user and in fact may have a high-powered computing facility totally within the confines of his or her office or laboratory. Many researchers in technology-oriented industries may develop personal computing systems (hardware, software, or both) that may be portable, thus allowing the employee to work at home. In other cases, networks of powerful processors may be in use as mail systems, general computers, and graphics generators. When many of the operators of such a system understand its most esoteric workings, the security of the information processed depends wholly on employee motivation and training.

Special and unusual information security standards are required for these environments. The standards must provide clearly defined statements of responsibility and must offer the research and engineering user a menu of security measures, and these measures must be acceptable in the working environment. These unique security needs follow from the job tasks in these activities. Some examples include

- The scientific programmer, who is using computers or computerlike devices to measure physical or chemical properties (analog signals may be collected and converted to digital signals for analysis or storage).
- The system development engineer, who may have custom-built operating computer models, testing devices, minicomputers, or terminal devices connected to interlaboratory or interplant systems.
- The scientist or engineer, who may have office computing through a desk minicomputer or sophisticated, intelligent terminal (can process locally) access to a central system.

In all these cases, remarkable differences exist from the traditional business systems case. The scientific or engineering user does not have systems development controls. If security measures are to be imbedded in the local processing system, the user or originator of the custom system or programs must build in the security elements.

There is unlikely to be formal media library services, so that if the data on disks and tapes are to be protected, the originator must provide that protection, logically or physically. Underlying these basic requirements is a supposition that the scientific or engineering user of personal work station computing is security conscious and motivated to protect company information. Such protection must rely on personal willingness to make value-factor decisions; for example, does it need protection, and to what degree? Suitable standards should provide guidance to this audience.

The security coordinator for the research and engineering divisions or departments plays a key role in developing these standards. An understanding and keen appreciation of the research and engineering environment, with the cooperation and contribution of personal computing systems users, are absolutely necessary.

Office Automation and Personal Computing

In this section we will deal with a phenomenon that poses a special threat—the appearance of personalized computing through terminals, intelligent office devices, minicomputers, and attached communications processors. A subset of this user group occurs on the next page. The rapid development of miniaturized computing facilities, with tremendous capabilities, is delivering electronic information access, withdrawal, and computing powers to individuals at work, at home, and while traveling. Vast networks for purposes of disseminating information are being constructed or are already in service. This threat is particularly serious because of two factors involving the users and the electronic information available:

1. The people who are using or will typically use personal computing facilities have the knowledge and capabilities to mount successful, clandestine attacks on critical electronic information databases. These are the high-grade knowledge workers, whose job requirements include detailed knowledge of one or more of the technical areas involved in the hardware and software construction of the information systems environment. In general, they must be assumed to be lacking only motivation for unauthorized activities—the capabilities are there.
2. The electronic information contained on network-connected systems may be sensitive. It includes financial analysis data, some in highly summarized form; research and development information; and, in advanced office systems, executive reports and correspondence.

The personalization of computing, implemented as local terminals or processors interconnected or as distributed computing (see discussion below), means that a large and varied population of users will have powerful equipment (in many cases ostensibly for entertainment or home uses), with potential for accessing important business information. An effective program for electronic information security may provide increasing protection as computing uses expand, but complete protection is probably impossible.

Business use of personal computing in its many forms means that not only do the authorized secretaries, managers, scientists, and engineers have access, but potential exists through common network connection for access by a wide range of hobbyists, home users, university people, and others. Increasing technical awareness leads to curiosity-driven or malicious attempts to access business files. Cases are on record of organized attempts by persons outside business to penetrate business computing networks for illegal purposes.

In this environment, the awareness and security consciousness of employees are most important, so that individually applied security measures will be effective. Logical security elements can limit penetrations by placing substantial barriers in the way of unauthorized people connected through networks. And properly applied encryption systems can provide robust security for the high-value information critical to a business (see earlier discussion).

Security managers should consider office automation as a part of the overall development and application of computing technology rather than as a separate phenomenon. This view helps to see how security measures previously applied to data centers and the use of computer terminals can be modified and adapted to office automation. It is also probably the most accurate viewpoint in terms of computing science.

Computers have been used for years to automate clerical, repetitive aspects of traditional office systems, such as accounts receivable, accounts payable, payrolls, general ledger, and personnel records. Office automation means that miniaturization and computing economics have now provided computers that are embedded in office systems hardware designed for personal, individual use. These new systems are designed to serve as personal, electronic substitutes for the administrative actions that have always required writing or printing on paper.

Office automation provides systems that electronically create messages, text, and graphics; that store and retrieve files; that communicate with other systems across the room or across the world; and that can produce paper copies anywhere. Security considerations in the use of such systems fall into two general categories. The first is the effect of the application of automated office systems on people, which may result in loss of traditional roles, poor morale, or antagonism. The second area for security concerns is in the technology itself, which presents unique security vulnerabilities for business information which is stored and moved about in electronic form.

Effects on People

These high-technology devices have implications equal in weight to those changes wrought by the computer in the 1960s. Managers must force rethinking of traditional business methods; systems analysts must open their minds to considering truly total systems, including the processing of written inputs or outputs at the ultimate user location, not just through the data center printer.

The most serious effect of these devices is not that of changes to procedure; rather, it is the modification of the job criteria for the human resource. Any good systems analyst knows that a system cannot be successfully installed unless the people who are to operate the system want it to work. Perhaps the worst approach is to promise too much when technology is installed. One can postulate a number of concerns that must be of interest to managers and systems analysts and, of course, security managers.

1. *The application of office technologies destroys the traditional (and sometimes professional) job positions in the office environment.* Past high-value office employees have been skilled generalists, understanding and responding to implied directives, keeping things going, and minding to countless details. Consider such work as filing, preparing correspondence, making travel reservations, sending out mail. How often has anyone seen procedures covering these things? The skilled office employee has learned to read subtle signs, to remember certain goals, and to use judgment to respond. The executive who says, "My secretary is wonderful," is really saying that the secretary has the best interests of the business at heart and responds to situations accordingly.

Technology does not allow for generalized responses and severely limits the application of judgmental decisions. So the office worker may have to change from a skilled generalist to a skilled technologist. Usually, this change will mean a narrower scope of work, but with more vertical depth. For example, where the clerical employee previously performed almost all the jobs in the office, that employee may now handle only communications, but may be involved from the initial dictation through the ultimate facsimile transmission and communication with the end recipient. This implies severe personal trauma for many who face these changes.

2. *Office technologies change the economic relationship of the employee to the job.* Investment in technology implies either greater throughput or lower operating costs, for otherwise the investment will not be made. In some cases, the application of technology will reduce the employee job content value and result in realignment of salary levels. One example of this is the automated duplicator. Previously, most companies used highly skilled printers to operate duplicating equipment, as setup and operation required fine tuning to achieve the proper mix of water, ink, paper, and pressure. The new duplicating equipment automatically senses when things go wrong and tells the operator in words just what to do about it. A low-grade clerical employee may easily be trained to operate one of these new machines.

3. *The use of high technology office systems may affect other functions as office procedure becomes more rigorously defined.* Consider the matter of filing of correspondence. When the office converts to a magnetic or microforms filing system, a secondary system must be provided for those functions and outside business not communicating in modes that are compatible. For example, a general counsel at a major corporation refused to accept any document in other than electronic (display) form. But since other departments and outside groups used paper mail, the lawyers of the company had to keep printers available.

4. *The development and availability of combination equipment having the characteristics of minicomputer, network-connected terminal, and typewriter means that many of the present skilled, intuitive, or decision-making activities in the office can be automated.* This will reduce the time required to do many

of the routine tasks and thus require fewer people. Those who remain will have to be able to operate and understand the systems involved. For example, travel reservations could be made directly with the airlines, with seat availability and confirmations appearing on the office terminal CRT.

All four concerns about office automation have security implications. These are not direct threats, such as that of software penetration, discussed below. Rather, they are implied threats developing from potential employee dissatisfaction or insecurity (see the earlier discussion on morale). The people who use automated office systems probably have personal characteristics that make them particularly interesting to the security manager. Typically, they

1. Are well educated and relatively young
2. Are above average in salary and potential
3. Have knowledge and capability to probe below the surface level of a system
4. Have no traditional constraints or controls in using the system, and those which do exist will be viewed by some as challenges
5. Are willing to take risks if an advantage is seen, with their greatest fear being that of embarrassment

This profile is the same as that of the typical "computer criminal."[24] Generally, business management does not recognize this threat or prefers to ignore it when it materializes.

Much of the information used in the office through personal computing is specially designed for use at decision-making levels of the business. For example, financial analysts may have access to central files of information that represent divisional or corporate "roll-ups" of year-to-date or monthly results. Executive secretaries have access to key memos concerning very private business matters, even when those memos are not directly addressed to them or their boss.

Concerns from Technology

The human vulnerabilities resulting from office automation are of concern to the security manager, but a more serious and immediate exposure results from technology. Fortunately, this area lends itself more readily to available security solutions than does the human factor. Technology centers around the electronic form of information, which no longer has the time and spatial constraints associated with information in paper forms. Vulnerabilities resulting from technology in the automated office environment may be considered as those resulting from communications, storage and retrieval, change of mode, operating systems, and expansion of the trusted group.

Communications. The capability to communicate information swiftly to any connected unit on a network or interconnected networks (almost all networks are by virtue of public utility services) is the essence of office automation. Time and spatial constraints associated with pieces of paper disappear, since information may be sent to distant places with no recognizable time lapse. Such service implies use of long lines or radio links, both of which represent a most serious vulnerability for business information. The solution for this exposure is encryption of transmitted information between the originating point and the addressee.

Within the business facility, physical security must be provided for the communications connections boxes, gateway computers, modems, or other equipment that might allow an unauthorized connection.

Storage and Retrieval.   Electronic office systems allow information in text or statistics form to be stored locally or at a central site for later retrieval or sending to others. Local storage may consist of writing on a magnetic disk, tape, or cartridge. Central storage may use either disk, tape, or cartridge but usually will employ on-line disks. Printing facilities may also have storage capabilities, if only for buffering purposes. All such magnetic storage causes security exposures. These risks occur because

- The magnetic media themselves may be stolen or temporarily removed for copying.
- Many systems offer the capability for transfer of information among various media stations from a remote site, through issuance of certain commands.
- Local storage may be susceptible to clandestine "dumping" of contents by unauthorized persons who may have technical capabilities for bypassing usual controls.

Protection for storage systems lies in effective application of logical security methods (discussed earlier in this chapter) that limit access to authorized system users and good physical security for tapes, disks, and cartridges that contain sensitive information.

Change of Mode.   Whenever information changes from human-readable form to electronic (digital or analog) forms, a security risk develops. This is so because at that moment the information exists in one place in both forms. Control is more complicated, and the opportunity for unauthorized change is ripe. Most cases of fraud result from unauthorized manipulation of a system at a point where information changes form, such as at a bank teller station or where an accounts receivable clerk is entering payments.

Another obvious exposure is in the office, when a secretary types a paper copy and at the same time enters an electronic record, perhaps for communication to a distant place. The information is then in four forms: the original, handwritten paper (if used), the ribbon for printing, the disk or cartridge used as storage of buffer, and the paper output. A good system is required to protect all these forms effectively, which will apply physical, logical, and encryption methods.

Operating Systems.   All complex office systems have operating systems, or executive systems, as either hardware electronics or program software loaded *onto* disks. Computer science has not yet been able to provide error-free "certified" operating systems, so that all software requires maintenance. This need is a security exposure, since it implies that parties outside the employee group authorized to use the system will have to understand and work on the controls for the systems. These controls in the operating system include the logical security features. Therefore, the systems maintenance activities may provide a miscreant the potential for bypassing security controls through manipulation of operating system software or hardware.

Protection in this circumstance is extremely difficult to provide with any certainty. Office systems users should make sure that service people have signed nondisclosure agreements and that people who work on systems are properly identified before the fact by their employer. In-house service people should be selected for their stability and reliability as well as for technical knowledge. This is easier said than done! All maintenance actions should be documented and the reasons for the work well understood by responsible managers. Unannounced maintenance should never be allowed.

Expansion of the Trusted Group.   This concern is directly related to the one above, since the requirement for servicing of electronic systems implies an enlargement of the usual trusted circle. For any piece of information, the originator has some finite audience in mind. Whether an executive memo, a note to your husband or wife, a Greek-language newspaper in New York City, or a whispered aside to a trusted associate, the originator has a limited information distribution intended. In physical or oral information passing, restriction of the audience is fairly simple. The weaknesses of the human memory are an effective limitation on orally passed information. Think of how often people use the term "I believe" when making a statement! Paper-based information can be controlled through the use of handwritten notes, sealed envelopes, registered mail, etc., although the copier has certainly put a chink in that armor!

Electronic information, especially with regard to interconnected office systems, is another matter. Information can be at two points thousands of miles apart, almost simultaneously. Ineffective control systems or system failures can result in misrouting of information with embarrassing results. Several cases are known where payroll information appeared unbidden and unwanted at distant printers in foreign businesses. Cases of "ghost" or stray data circulating through networks are not uncommon.

Intentional or chance penetrations through manipulation of the system during maintenance of hardware or software is not unlikely. Consider the case where a defect in a magnetic medium (tape or disk) requires the maintenance person to attempt retrieval of information. This is another evident case where the information will be exposed to an outsider in the course of authorized activity.

There are many circumstances wherein unauthorized activity, perhaps in conjunction with routine servicing, could result in information exposures. Since office information tends to be in more finished form, the penetrator gets more for his or her effort if the target is well planned.

Another aspect of the vulnerabilities resulting from an enlargement of the trusted circle and system software involves the concept of "distributed computing." Originally, computers operated at only one location. Then terminals allowed connection to distant points, where users could share the computing power. Each computer, however, had a unique operating system with varying features that made interconnect and data interchange difficult or impossible. Distributed computing means that a series of interconnected computers share the same executive or operating system, thus being able to exchange information and services as though many were one. This also means that operating systems changes, and hence changes to security controls, may potentially be made to all units from a distant station. Good procedures and administrative controls for systems changes and user recognition of such changes are important to maintain system integrity.

Some distributed office systems use coaxial cable as a sort of "data pipe," transmitting all messages or information to all stations. The correct station (as addressee) sorts out the messages intended by examining the addressee codes and rejecting those messages for other stations. If a station can be clandestinely attached to this cable, the potential exists for copying off all traffic and examining same at leisure. Cables should therefore be protected the same as any other hardware. They should not go outside control of the using business. Where connections are made to public utility lines, encryption is the security solution.

Manufacturing Systems

Computer-aided manufacturing has made great strides in recent years. Special local area network and processing technologies have been developed by General Motors Corporation and others to aid in the automation and resulting efficiencies of manufacturing processes. Generally, these systems relate to computer-driven tools, reporting and analysis of work in process, control of robotics, time accounting and cost control, and quality control systems. Most of these in-plant systems do not require extensive security. However, a company should be concerned about information integrity, and so some reasonable level of systems security is required. Further, summary reports may be sensitive and may require appropriate control over documents and print files. Centralized minicomputers or microcomputers in a plant setting require physical security to ensure reliability and to protect against tampering.

Data Processing and Telecommunications

Although a data center is different in mission and scope from a telecommunications center, both have computers and both process information. In some cases, the similarities outweigh the differences, especially where large data traffic network switches are in operation. In these environments, the responsible management must deal with electronic security in two modes. First, access to data through the physical facilities of the data center or telecommunications center must be controlled. That is, access to information on tapes, disks, or cartridges, and access through terminals of other connection devices internal to the data center must be strictly and severely controlled. Usually this means that, in addition to the usual controls over physical entry to the plant, certain areas inside the building must be further restricted. These usually include the operations area (where consoles are located), disk, tape, and cartridge storage and use areas, output processing areas (paper and microforms), and communications equipment rooms. Second, logical access control resources must be provided on a "menu" basis to the customers of the data processing and telecommunication service activities. These should consist of

- Additional restrictions on the handling or processing of information with a value factor assigned, available as optional steps when required by the customer.
- Logical security subsystems (e.g., file, record, or data element passwording capabilities), which may be selected and applied at the user's discretion.
- Encryption systems, implemented as hardware or software, for use when information sensitivity dictates.

A most important observation here: the data center or telecommunications manager provides some standard level of security to meet routine needs. Incremental security elements, applied for high-value-factor information at user request, are the responsibility of the functional manager using the data processing or telecommunications service (and may be paid for by that manager).

For a long time, business people looked to the data processing manager to make security decisions on information processed and to implement those decisions within the area of responsibility. This begs the question of the security of that same information in hardcopy form outside the data center. Real security for information requires a recognition and acceptance of responsibility by the originator and functional users of the information. The data processing and telecommunications functions are service activities and cannot be expected to generate decisions concerning information sensitivity. Effective protection for information occurs only when management (user?) demands the necessary security from the data processing and telecommunications activities and from direct information users outside those areas.

The Menu

By establishing a standard set of security features, the information processing operations can limit the variety of security measures required and requested. A listing of these offerings, published for the users in a menu format, encourages their use and establishes a justification requirement should additional or different protection be requested.

Physical Offerings

Input processing: all batches can be processed and moved with covers and receipted at each step. *Output processing:* printers and micromation units can be segregated by means of screens or restricted areas during the processing of certain runs. Reports can be stamped, overprinted, specially covered, numbered, packaged, etc., to provide positive control and limit exposure. Generally, these measures would tie into established company policies regarding marking and handling of high-value-factor information.

Logical Offerings

These subsystems, usually appended to or part of the operating system, allow various levels of access control, at the option of the user. Examples are the IBM RAC-F package, Computer Associate's ACF-2, and DEC's VAX/VMS operating system features.

A user or data owner may choose to have files "public," at one end of the security spectrum or to establish controls down to the data element level. Generally, the more recent software packages offer increasing flexibility and protection. VMS, for example, offers very powerful protection tools (the effectiveness of any package depends on the user's willingness to apply it properly).

Each data processing center should have a security coordinator with suitable skills to control and monitor the security subsystem and its environment. Generally, the tasks consist of interface with the systems maintenance activity and with the data processing users. The user management must indicate (preferably in writing to ensure accountability) those access authorizations needed for business purposes. The data processing security coordinator and staff then make user-authorized changes to access authorization tables in the security subsystem. This activity includes installation and maintenance of the security subsystem's software, often with some vendor assistance. There may be a significant workload in the effort. A large corporate data center may require four to five people on the security staff.

The implementing of access management decisions, in many cases, has moved to the user's office. Modern access management systems allow the functional user to make access authorization changes directly, through a terminal, to the security subsystem. This of course recognizes the point made above; that is, that the data center or telecommunications manager is only responding to user security requirements.

Telecommunications Risk Environments

Many security exposures exist in telecommunications systems and applications. In any modern, worldwide company, all time-sensitive information is transmitted electronically. Such transmissions offer tempting targets to industrial espionage agents and, more important, are susceptible to those elements of society intent on mischief. In this group are employees seeking satisfaction or profit, groups with political ends, and organized crime.

Business vulnerabilities fall into two general areas. The most severe risk is that of the loss of information integrity, privacy, or availability due to actions of employees. A second and lesser risk is from exposure of information to damage or destruction because of the acts of outsiders. Both areas of vulnerability occur in these risk environments: (1) the environment wherein information form is changed and (2) the environment in which information is in transmission.

Risk Environment 1—Change of Form.   Information changes form when it is converted from human-use format to machine-use format. For example, human voice is changed to analog signal when one speaks into a telephone or feeds paper into a facsimile transmitter. A form change also occurs when data are transcribed from paper to a keyboard-initiated signal or from a scanned printed format to electronic signals. The result of all this activity is, similarly, a change of form, which is called *output.*

In this risk environment, security is usually compromised because of eavesdropping (unauthorized listening) or unauthorized observation. In essence, this risk environment calls for proper physical protections (door locks, restricted areas, screening) and good procedure (do not discuss classified information on the telephone in a public place; keep documents covered; restrict access to documents).

Risk environment 1 is not a case for technical security measures, except in the rare instance where shielding to prevent emission pickup from conversations might be desirable. This is a general case and not directly related to telecommunications.

Risk Environment 2—Information Transmission.   Information is in transmission continually, in electronic form, through hardware or radio (microwave) circuits. Included in these circuits are switching centers and junction boxes. Circuits carrying information travel through physical areas that must be considered hostile. They are outside the control of the business user. They are also subject to simple, easy, and relatively cheap interception. Information-carrying circuits include public telephone lines and microwave links. Both may be tapped or intercepted. Traffic may be recorded and analyzed in depth, at leisure, and such activity requires only a modest investment in terms of potential values.

Telephone and data link switching centers and connection boxes offer simple, easy-to-access physical connection points for temporary and long-term eavesdropping or copying of voice and data traffic. Many of these physical elements are outside the control of the using business, and even those within a company's facilities are often poorly protected. In most cases, these elements are maintained by the employees of other companies and so offer tempting targets for would-be intelligence gatherers.

Security Measures

In all cases of vulnerability described, primary security rests with effective protection of facilities. That is, effective management and restrictions of access to, and operation on, communications facilities under business user control, and good procedure on handling information at change-of-form locations. Secondary protection, that which would safeguard information in transmission, requires data transformation or encryption of traffic; that is, all high-value-factor communications traffic, including voice and facsimile, must be transformed using an encryption algorithm. This may be accomplished through installed hard-wired hardware, software, or hand-held partial-message encryption devices. The four levels of security apply.

Before such measures for technical protection can be used, two prerequisites must be met:

1. Technology must be available to make the protection reasonable and cost-efficient in the business situation.
2. Managers using the telecommunications facilities must believe that the risk exists and that it justifies the effort of protection.

Encryption technology is fast developing and is available today to cover all the risks, except in a few cases (e.g., dial-up timesharing). But current technology is expensive and detracts from the convenience usually expected by users (see the earlier discussion of encryption element).

Voice-encryption hardware is expensive but is now fairly convenient to use. Convenience and ease of use are directly related to cost. Hand-encryption devices (word encryptors) are inconvenient but relatively cheap and portable.

Current software products have high overhead costs. Hardware is effective only on a link basis but is fast becoming economical.

Acceptance of the risk and need for protection are fairly low. Most managers do not really believe that their communications are seriously exposed. However, cases of telecommunications interceptions for purposes of crime or mischief demonstrate that encrypting links carrying volumes of sensitive traffic can pose a major security problem. The training of employees in awareness of voice communications exposures should be mandatory.

Timesharing and Distributed Computing

Networked (timesharing and distributed) computing is a closely related manifestation of one phenomenon. That is, people want to have computing power close to their personal business activities whenever it will help do the job. Timesharing refers to the connection of multiple terminals to a central processor, where the speed and capacity of the central computer make the service to each user appear to be immediate. Distributed computing has the same effect, except that in this case each individual user has a processor that may or may not be connected to a central computer but that is always connected to a network joining several similar units. Local area networks are common forms of distributed computing.

Characteristics

Important characteristics of timesharing and distributed computing for electronic information security are as follows:

1. Protection must rely on logical security methods, using hardware or software implementations, since these modes deliver computing power to many and remote locations (especially severe vulnerabilities in the case of "dial-up" services.
2. Personal identification is difficult and costly, since physical presence at an identity checkpoint is not practical. The systems must rely on identification-authentication systems, which are unreliable due to human failure.
3. Security depends heavily on individual system users accepting and complying with good security practices (e.g., keeping passwords private).
4. Since files may be created outside established structures (e.g., as with individuals using APL programming), access to supposedly private files may be gained through file design flaws or through failure of the creator or user to apply protective features.

The security coordinator serving a population of timesharing or distributed (office systems or LANs) computing users has a large task in employee education and motivation. Since good policy and standards will require the data center or computing system designer to offer security alternatives, protection ultimately depends on the personal acceptance of security responsibility by every user of the system. The security coordinator, in this case, may also be called on to offer advice in setting up files and access control methods. To do this, a competence in technology in addition to a good grasp of security methods is needed.

Logical Security Elements

Logical security elements are those permiting the identification and authentication of a user, followed by authorization to do certain preordained things (see a file, execute a program, modify a data element, etc.). In the traditional case, the logical security elements are supported and complemented by physical security elements. For example, the employee must gain access to the building and to the terminal room before "signing on." In the timesharing-distributed computing situation, however, the user may be thousands of miles away. Logical security must then take up the slack in control caused by the inability of the security system to provide a physical check.

Various methods are available. Current technology is developing prototype hand geometry measurement devices and voice recognition systems. More commonplace are the ubiquitous passwords, which for any degree of robustness must be combined with an authentication. This may be done by the users providing an answer to one of a series of preset questions (e.g., what is your mother-in-law's maiden name?) or by requiring the entry of a date-related data item that, with the password, combines to form a valid authentication.

The third protective element of the logical security blanket is authorization. This means that once identification and authentication are successfully completed, the user is limited through computer reference to a table (or similar method) to certain functions or files. Obviously, this not only limits what the authorized user may do, but it restricts the potential damage from a successful penetrator to only one portion of the data files.

Systems with only one of the three logical security elements are commonplace, but sadly undependable. The security coordinator must understand the exposures and be prepared to recommend reasonable implementations of measures that fit the sensitivity or value factor of the data.

In the early stages of the electronic information security program, a large expenditure of human resources and funds may be anticipated in the area of timesharing and distributed computing. Most of this will be for the development and administration of logical security elements.

PROGRAM THEORY SUMMARY

The three-dimensional matrix (see Figure 7.1) illustrates the program theory. In essence, the suggested information security program is based on well-defined structure; businesswide applicability across all functions; effective protection through security elements applied in concentric levels, according to information valuation. The three-dimensional matrix can be used to view the program concept as a series of management actions. Each intersect of the three planes represents a directive and a set of reactions. For example, consider the intersect of the planes of executive program direction, office automation, and logical protection. Executive program direction is policy that may state that information is limited to those employees having a need to know. Office automation is a fairly unstructured environment typically using some form of distributed computing. Logical protection includes the security elements required for access management (personal identification, authentication, and authorization) and encryption.

At this intersect, executive program direction or policy should establish the requirement for protection of information at each of the potential valuations (e.g., registered, private, employee confidential, or similar). The policy must accommodate an environment such as office automation. It probably does this through general statements. Appropriate logical protection elements for the office situation must be described in a standard (another plane). The policy establishes the need for such a standard, so the reaction to the directive at this intersect is development of a standard for office automation.

At other intersections of the matrix planes, similar actions can be postulated. Actual implementation of the program is more direct, since the development and publication of policy, standards, and procedures provide an action framework. The evolution of the framework for a particular business is the natural result of a series of processes, called the program. The following sections and chapters outline these processes in the rough sequence of actual occurrence, although some overlap necessarily happens.

The potential threat to digital electronic information is widely dispersed over a large, diverse population. Would-be penetrators may be attacking from varied environments, using many different systems and without regard to physical location or distance. The traditional security program, addressing the data center as the locus for concern, will not suffice. The security program for the 1990s must have

- *Catholicity*—the program must address all the various applications and circumstances of computer system use in the business.
- *Flexibility*—the program must provide for reasonable management decisions in light of business requirements while offering some generally acceptable level of protection.

The electronic information security program suggested by the matrix in Figure 7.1 provides a flexible, encompassing program with a dynamic management control process. This is a program attuned to the 1990s business environment.

EIGHT

Practical Application
of Information
Management Concepts

METRICS FOR AN EFFECTIVE PROGRAM

Managers can apply the following set of four metrics to determine whether an information security program is effective.

1. The program requirements must be *simple* or, at worst, be able to be explained simply. Since most employees will not perceive security to be a major part of job responsibilities, security requirements must be simple and easy to follow. Complex instructions will not be remembered or, worse, will not be read at all and will be rejected out of hand.

2. Information security processes must be *practical* in terms of the work situation. Security must be defined so as not to interfere with the employees' completion of assigned tasks. For example, a requirement that routine documents circulated among hundreds of employees be individually logged and controlled is not practical; in such a case, the classification is probably wrong.

3. Information security process and rules must *fit* the company's operating and organizational practices. If the business is decentralized, as many routine information security processes as are practical should be left to local definition. If the business has many diverse operations (a conglomerate), information security practices may be completely different for various parts of the company.

4. Information security investments must be based on *business decisions*. There are no "golden tablets" handed down from on high to identify the rules for information security. Rather, security is a business process and should be based on management's risk acceptance posture derived from careful consideration of estimated information risks and protection costs.

ORGANIZATION AND DIRECTION

The organization selected for managing information depends on company organization and operating practices. However, we can generalize and suggest a set of information jobs, with related tasks, and an organization structure to fit most businesses. The important point is that if a company wants to manage the information resource, it cannot just add the information tasks to some existing job, such as systems director, because this is a critical activity. A company would not ask the vice-president of finance to manage human resources on the side. Information is equally important.

Job Titles

Although job titles and task descriptions may vary, as appropriate to business circumstances, these are the generic information management titles:

> Vice-President, Information Resources (Information Executive)
> > Information Resource Manager
> > > Data Administration Manager
> > > Information Security Manager*
> > Information Systems Manager
> > > Systems Development Manager
> > > Systems and Communications Operations Manager
> > > Information Technology Manager

These jobs are oriented toward helping the information executive fulfill his or her primary role: to develop and deliver information that will serve as a strategic catalyst and synergistic opportunity for the business.

Task Definitions

Information Executive

This position

- Reports to the CEO
- Advises executive management on use of information resources and recommends business opportunities flowing from the development of information resources

---

*May report to Corporate Security Manager.

- Improves internal operations efficiencies through delivery of quality information
- Adds value to business operations by synergistic use of information resources

Information Resource Manager

This position

- Reports to the information executive
- Manages the company's information inventory
- Works closely with functional information owners to classify information and to control information applications
- Maintains a data dictionary and ensures interface standardization and compatibility among the company's basic information elements
- Obtains authorization from information owners for information use
- Issues authorizations to develop new information elements as required for business operations
- Performs analysis and cost studies to minimize overall costs of the company's information base

Data Administration Manager

This position

- Reports to the information resource manager
- Controls the information base for the company
- Maintains a data dictionary showing the technical characteristics of the company's primary data elements
- Manages the identification and formatting of new data elements authorized by information owners
- Provides technical assistance to systems development activities
- Coordinates, and obtains approval for, data applications

Information Security Manager

This position

- Reports to the company security manager (recommended) or to the information resource manager
- Works with information owners to properly classify company information elements
- Develops protective measures and coordinates these with systems developers, information owners, and information users
- Provides advice and technical assistance, including information security plans and staff training materials
- Works with the technology manager to identify appropriate logical security measures for computer systems and telecommunications systems

Information Systems Manager

This position

- Reports to the information executive
- Directs the development of business information systems in both computerized and manual forms
- Supervises the overall operations of information processing and telecommunications
- Improves efficiency and reduces costs for information operations by identifying and applying the most appropriate technology
- Provides financial management of the information infrastructure, computers, communications lines, data centers, and so forth
- Establishes standards for decentralized use of computers and communications services
- Provides services to individual information users (executive information center and so forth)

Systems Development Manager

This position

- Reports to the information systems manager
- Is responsible for the development, programming, testing, installation, and maintenance of approved business systems applications
- Coordinates with the information systems manager to ensure proper control and conservation of the company information resource
- Develops and installs controls to ensure quality information
- Provides services and support to individual systems developers

Systems and Communications Operations Manager

This position

- Reports to the information systems manager
- Manages and directs the operation of centralized data processing centers and telecommunications networks
- Coordinates with technology manager to ensure the availability of technical facilities to meet established standards
- Applies security software controls as designated by the information security manager

Information Technology Manager

This position

- Researches and identifies current information technologies
- Recommends technologies appropriate or advantageous to the company

- Coordinates on selection of logical security control systems with the information security manager
- Advises systems developers and individual systems users
- Establishes technology standards for the company to ensure consistency in information interchanges and to minimize costs

Figure 8.1 shows an organization chart including information management jobs.

A MANAGEMENT INFORMATION AUDIT

For the company that has not previously considered information resource management, an information audit checklist is a valuable tool. Here, we suggest two such checklists:

1. An initial information management audit, which should lead to management decisions and actions to establish a program, identify the company's information base, and begin the process of information control

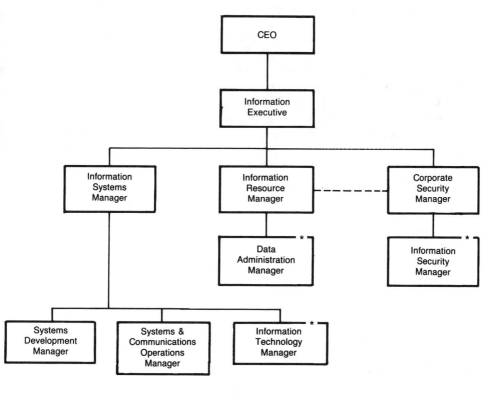

*Close working relationship.

Figure 8.1   Information management concept for business organization.

2. A routine information audit, one which could be used at regular intervals (perhaps by the company's auditors) once an information management program is established and working

Initial Information Management Audit

The questions are sequentially cumulative in effect; that is, if the answer to number 2 is yes, number 3 should logically follow from that base. In many cases, the requirements of the earlier questions will have been met, but the following details may be lacking. All the requirements should be considered necessary for an effective information management program.

1. Has executive management assigned a senior manager the responsibility for information management?
2. Has a company policy been published establishing the base information management requirements, including company classifications and minimal protection?
3. Are company information classification definitions established, and are employees trained on using these?
4. Has the company identified its critical information elements, and have classification decisions been made for these?
5. Have procedures regarding information protection been published, and do employees follow them?
6. Do information protection procedures cover all forms of information?
7. Do information protection procedures provide for computer and manual processing?
8. Has an information owner been assigned responsibility for each basic information element?
9. Are initial information classification decisions made by the information owners?
10. Do procedures facilitate decisions on classification and protection of new company information at origination?
11. Are records retention procedures in place to control storage costs and avoid legal exposures, and do these procedures cover all information forms?
12. Are business recovery plans written to ensure that critical information will continue to be available should a disaster occur? The responsibility for protection of business resources should rest with one manager. This is appropriately the company security manager. Information security should not be assigned to the information systems function.
13. Does the company security department have assigned resources to allow the fulfillment of information protection responsibilities (e.g., information security manager)? The security function must have sufficient expertise to al-

low the definition of required protection methods for all forms of information. (This does not mean that security software implementation cannot be done by information systems specialists.)

14. Has the security manager established the necessary working relationships with functions associated with information protection afforts (e.g., information systems technology, general counsel, audit, comptroller, administration)? The security function must be a part of the ongoing company information management process.

15. Do company policies define the purpose and ground rules for managing information resources, including information protection? Policy should define all critical requirements but should not include procedural matters.

16. Do information protection policies acknowledge the legal purposes (i.e., protection and conservation of proprietary information) of the company's information protection program? Court decisions make it clear that a formal, effective, and active information protection program is necessary if a company is to assert its rights to proprietary information (*Motorola Inc. vs. Fairchild Camera and Instrument Corp.*, D. Ariz. 1973, 366 F. Supp. 1173).

17. Do company information management policies provide for a controlled acceptance of risk? Information protection is not an absolute; business requirements may dictate that certain risks be taken. Such risk-taking should be acknowledged, controlled, and approved by senior management.

18. Is the information policy supported by published information protection standards that cover all aspects of company operations involving information creation, employee handling, transmittal, communication, processing, storage, and destruction? Information protection standards are the cohesive force in a program for network security. The standards provide the instructions for all employees involved with information resources.

19. Do information protection standards include instructions for identifying, classifying, marking, handling, and protecting information in all forms? Comprehensive standards are important; protection of one form of information and disregard for others is really no protection at all.

20. Are information protection standards published in forms that are appropriate and useful to the various employee groups or classes? Instructions must be made available in forms convenient for use. Secretaries do not need the entire standards package, but their work usually involves much valuable information. A booklet addressed to secretaries might be effective.

21. Do information protection standards address all facets of the company's computing and networking infrastructure? The entire company information processing environment must be covered by standards; the weak link will be the place where the leak occurs.

22. Do information protection standards cover all employee aspects of the use of the company's computer and telecommunications resources? Today we are seeing an information explosion; people are using computer terminals and making telephone calls everywhere, even on airplanes and trains. All these risks must be covered in the standards.

23. Do information standards fix clearly the responsibilities of the various employee classes and groups (e.g., managers, supervisors, employees, terminal users, secretaries, personal computer users, etc.)? Each employee must be able to recognize a clear responsibility for taking action to protect company information.

24. Do information protection standards address the company's information interchanges with suppliers, customers, outside counsel, business partners, and foreign countries? Every business passes information to outsiders and receives information from outsiders. These exchanges are being automated, and many now take place electronically for reasons of efficiency and economy. There is a severe risk in such activities when company networks become involved.

25. Do information protection standards cover interconnection with outside networks and data communications services? The use of public data services, airlines reservation systems, and value-added carriers may involve some risk to company information resources. Such connections should be evaluated by the security function before a decision for their use is made.

26. Do information protection standards cover the use of company networks by authorized outsiders? For good business reasons, most companies will sooner or later allow outside parties to use the company's networks. Care should be taken to define these outside parties' rights and obligations and to control their access and activities. A lawsuit after a breach of trust is not really a remedy once information has been exposed.

27. Are information security standards covering the production and distribution of documents followed in all company offices and reproduction centers?

28. Do secretaries have current information protection requirements instructions, and are they followed scrupulously? Secretaries are key people in establishing effective information protection practices.

29. Are conflict of interest agreements and disclosure agreements used when appropriate to protect mental information? When company information is provided to employees or contractors, a contract may provide legal remedy should a trust be abused. Agreements define the responsibilities of the parties and, most important, help establish the company's rights to its information.

30. Is high-value information controlled and tracked throughout its life cycle?

A Routine Information Management Audit

The following checklist can be used for periodically reviewing the status of an information management program. The answers assure management that the basic building blocks of the program are in place and the controls functioning.

---

1. Has executive management assigned a senior manager the responsibility for information management?
2. Has a company policy been published establishing the base information management requirements, including company classifications and minimal protection?
3. Are company information classification definitions established, and are employees trained on using these?
4. Has the company identified its critical information elements, and have classification decisions been made for these?
5. Have procedures regarding information protection been published, and do employees follow them?
6. Do information protection procedures cover all forms of information?
7. Do information protection procedures provide for computer and manual processing?
8. Has an information owner been assigned responsibility for each basic information element?
9. Are initial information classification decisions made by the information owners?
10. Do procedures facilitate decisions on classification and protection of new company information at origination?
11. Are records retention procedures in place to control storage costs and avoid legal exposures, and do these procedures cover all information forms?
12. Are business recovery plans written to ensure that critical information will continue to be available should a disaster occur?

GETTING STARTED

An established policy is the foundation for the information security program. The next step is to develop detailed policy implementation requirements that are reasonably applicable across the company.

The corporate manager of information security and the unit security coordinators share responsibility for developing policy requirements. For our purposes we will call these *standards*. Standards are the second level in the three-level policy structure shown in the three-dimensional matrix in Figure 7.1.

The corporate manager and the unit security coordinators form a committee, which uses the published policy and their knowledge and skills to research and build the set of implementing measures or standards. A set of such standards is provided in Appendix 2 and forms the guidelines for operating unit action to meet policy intent.

The first draft, or the earliest agreed form, of the standards should be used by the security coordinators to perform a unit security requirements survey, described in the following pages. This survey allows management a look at the effort and cost that will be involved. Planning and budgeting for one or more years, in terms of what effort will be required to meet the policy, follow from the requirements survey. The survey will provide detailed information about the circumstances in each operating unit, thus serving as a good "sounding board" for further review and evaluation of the standard.

Within a reasonable time of publication of the first draft of the standard, and somewhat concurrent with completion of the requirements survey, the final, authoritative standard should be published. The standards then become the "target" for program actions; the requirements survey tools may be used again periodically as a security review method.

Security Requirements Survey

This "Requirement Survey" is based on the newly published Standards for Electronic Information Security. The survey is conducted by the unit security coordinators. The approach, method, and effort to be put into the requirements survey depend on the nature of the unit being surveyed. Since the outcome of the survey will form the basis for planning program-implementing actions, the survey must be in enough detail to allow credible planning activities.

In a large technologic organization, such a survey may require six months' time. An engineering group would be typical, where many computers are used and where unique circumstances, such as computer laboratories, may require special consideration. Comparatively, a marketing organization, operating through local sales offices, might be able to base the security requirements survey entirely on the headquarters and one typical branch.

These variations accent the importance of the unit security coordinator's familiarity with unit operations. In one actual case, the unit security coordinators prepared a survey form, collected information, and then wrote a series of computer programs to summarize and analyze survey data. This unit, it was discovered, had over a thousand computers in use! The process of conducting the security requirements survey in an operating unit may follow various paths, but generally the activities may be broken down into four phases.

Phase 1

The unit security coordinator will have participated in the development of the information security standards. It may be assumed that the standards are relevant to the unit and its operating mode. In phase 1, the security coordinator considers the application of the standards to the operating unit. Some portions may be considered to be fully accomplished; physical security in data centers is usually such an item. Other requirements may need further development or explanation before conducting the survey. Such an item might be encryption, since most businesses are not yet involved in its use.

During phase 1, then, the security coordinator develops a survey rationale suitable to the various security elements and their current status in his or her unit. The survey rationale may include such subject categories as

- Fully accomplished, requirements survey not needed, coordinator can evaluate situation personally
- Partially in place, survey need only ask appropriate question
- Not widely understood, concept introduction required as presurvey
- New item to unit, training required before survey respondents can reply intelligently

Phase 2

The security coordinator should now be ready to prepare the survey vehicle. This may be a report to be prepared directly by the security coordinator, a personal survey based on visits to appropriate people and places, a mailed questionnaire, or any combination of these. Unit size, geographic dispersion of activities, technologic complexity and diversity, and unit organization structure will bear on the survey vehicle selection. Appendix 4 illustrates a detailed requirements survey form, designed for a specific application—the reader should modify to fit needs.

The use of a survey form is recommended. Such a form, as a questionnaire or fill-in sheet, ensures that all subjects are covered and that a written record of the responses is developed. This will be important later on in the program when on going program management requires that accomplishments be tracked against requirements.

Phase 3

This phase is the actual survey itself. A cover memo from a senior unit manager should ask, "What must be done to bring the unit into compliance with the Information Security Standards?" It is important to keep this in mind as the survey progresses. The relative difficulty of cost associated with compliance should be noted as part of the survey process but is not relevant to answering the question. In other words, do not allow respondents to answer questions by merely saying, "It is too expensive." The ability or willingness of management to pay for compliance is a part of the postsurvey process. The requirements survey must provide information on which management can base decisions to invest or to take risks.

The security coordinator, in conducting the survey, should act as impartially and objectively as possible. Management support for the security requirements survey, as discussed previously, is essential. At a minimum, the survey should answer these questions for each security element stipulated by the Information Security Standards:

- What are the difficulties foreseen?
- Is the technology required available?
- What will the total cost be?
- What timing constraints will delay compliance?

Phase 4

Once the information from the survey is collected, it must be assembled, collated, analyzed, and presented to unit management. The level of detail to be presented depends on local management practice, but sufficient understanding must be offered so that unit managers can intelligently present unit decisions to corporate executives.

The output from the requirements survey is the business plan. This plan identifies the existing shortfalls versus the Information Security Standards and specifies the actions, resources, spending, and timing of the unit's proposed actions to meet the standards. In most cases, unit or division management will look to the security coordinator to propose a plan. It may be well for the security coordinator to review a draft of the plan proposed with the corporate manager of electronic security.

The business plan (regenerated per the organization's planning cycle) then represents a commitment to action. Annual security spending plans will be based, in part, on remaining or new compliance items.

Risk Analysis

We have all heard about market research that indicated that there was no market for such-and-such, but when the determined entrepreneur brought the product to market anyhow, he or she made a million dollars. The same judgments must be applied to risk analysis. We would prefer to be able to present senior managers with economic values representing our business risk with and without an information security program. To date, efforts to do so have been compromised by

- A lack of actual case data on which to base probability estimates, resulting in the use of "learned judgments" and raising serious questions as to validity;
- A tendency to overlook serious (unforeseen) risk and to emphasize lesser exposures, simply because the "crime technology" is so new;
- Excessive costs to perform an effective risk analysis, if such is possible, may not appear justified by the reliability of the results;
- A tendency to address the form of information (computer form) rather than the asset itself (information in *any* form).

Computer information processing in an organization of any significant size is a complex and technical matter. Managers trying to determine what to do to ensure some acceptable level of computing security are faced with a bewildering problem. The potential sources and types of attack on computing systems appear endless. Total protection is prohibitively expensive. The established security organization is not usually equipped (or chartered) to deal with the matter. What to do? A risk analysis may be called for. Many proposals for a highly structured probability-based risk analysis have been made. Software packages are for sale, and the U.S. Bureau of Standards has published a procedure.

For the large company, a businesswide, rigorous risk analysis using currently fashionable methods is probably impractical. This is true because the number of exposures and the number of information processes are too great to be handled by any method claiming precision. The popular risk analysis methods have serious flaws, addressed below, that compromise the credibility of the results and make the considerable cost of such analysis a dubious bargain (*Business Week*, April 20, 1981, estimated $250,000 for a risk analysis for a $1 billion company).

For limited situations, such as a case where management wishes to know whether to accept a risk—perhaps because protection appears too costly—risk analysis of a general or rigorous nature may be worthwhile. Such an application might be one that involves a single system, say an order entry system using terminals at sales branches. The present mathematics-based risk analysis methods are less likely to become bogged down in masses of information, thus making the "fatal flaws" more manageable. Currently, several attractive risk analysis packages, running on PCs, are available and useful in a constrained application.

Most of the risk analysis methods deal most effectively with what might be called "disasters"—that is, the risk of fire, flood, or other destruction of processing capabilities. These are not trivial but are not the primary concern here, not being within the definition of electronic information security. Building safety is important to information security—if the building is destroyed by fire, the information is gone—but facility safety systems are a separate matter, if for no other reason than to keep the subject within reasonable scope.

A general set of methods and procedures is applied by all the structured mathematics-based risk analysis methods studied. Certain differences occur— some are implemented through computer programs—but the approach is fairly standardized.

Since most rigorous risk analysis proposals envision an analysis for an entire organization (an approach that is invalid, in my opinion), a committee is set up. The committee provides a range of knowledge about the business systems, activities, facilities, processes, and methods that must be considered in the analysis. The committee might include the systems group, the functional user group, computer operations, facilities maintenance, and so on. The committee applies its overall knowledge to developing the data for the risk analysis (which is essentially an application of probability theory).

Next, the committee lists all the vulnerabilities occurring as the systems and information processes proceed in the course of business. The committee assigns risk values, in terms of dollars, pounds sterling, or whatever, to each potential vulnerability event.

Now, the committee must estimate the possibility, or probability, of each event occurring. (Since there could be thousands of items in each of these categories, this is not a small undertaking!)

The conclusion of the study is a process of multiplying risk values by probability factors, to get an exposure cost. This exposure cost, or decision value, is then used by management to decide when and where to spend on security. (Often it is used by security people to try to convince management to spend.)

Details of Risk Analysis

In a large corporation, with multiple divisions spread over wide geographic areas, the risk analysis committee must be large. Probably the committee would consist of division or area subcommittees. The size of the task of identifying the individual vulnerability-causing business activities is mind-boggling. Consider one function, accounts receivable. A look at such a function shows that vulnerabilities occur (1) whenever information changes form, as from paper to digital, or is transmitted through communications circuits, and (2) whenever information is moved interorganizationally or functionally, as when an order is processed from accounts receivable through to commissions files. The potential vulnerability points in such a system, in a large business, could be in the hundreds. Total vulnerability points in the operations of a large corporation could be in the tens of thousands.

The committee's task, then, is a huge one. Without knowledgeable, capable people, the committee cannot do its job. If knowledgeable, capable people are assigned, they will be tied up for a long time. The conclusion is that popular risk analysis methods are costly. The fatal flaws in the method should raise serious doubts about the justification of that cost.

The popular mathematical methods of risk analysis, unless contrained severely in scope, have serious or fatal flaws. As discussed above under cost, the potential numbers of vulnerability points may be very large. The first fatal flaw arises from this fact. The fatal flaw is that *the committee is very likely to overlook a serious vulnerability*.

A security program tied to a committee's listing of required protection points, with the potential for omissions, cannot be considered an acceptable program. A general approach using information valuation is preferable.

The second fatal flaw in risk analysis is in the development of probability. The insurance industry uses a mortality table or other actual experience records to develop estimates of risk. No such historical data are available to the risk analysis committee. The probability assigned to each vulnerability point, that is, the likelihood of a security breach occurring at that point, is arrived at by consensus of the committee members. *Webster's New Collegiate Dictionary* says this is a "guess," i.e., "forming an opinion from little or no evidence." Using this method, a vulnerability estimated as a million-to-one shot may occur three times in the next year, while a one-in-ten estimated probability may never occur. Thus the second fatal flaw is that *the probability estimates' value will range from dubious to worthless*.

A risk value must be developed for each potential vulnerability; for example, should the payroll file be compromised; what will it cost us? Generally, current risk analysis methods recognize the fallibility of this estimation. A typical approach is to apply order-of-magnitude values; for example, the risk is $1,000,

$10,000, $100,000, $1,000,000, etc. The third fatal flaw is obvious: *The values assigned may be in error by an order of magnitude.*

The data generated by the committee during the activities described are now used to compute decision base results. These results, in the form of dollar figures, are purported to represent the risk involved in a vulnerability point. Management will then make decisions on computing security investments based on these decision base values. The decision base value is computed as follows:

(value of event) times (probability of event) equals (decision base value)

or

$$Ve \times Pe = DBV$$

A very large array of events and risk values should result from the committee's work. The fatal flaws noted call into question the completeness and value of the data. Consider the listing in terms of the fatal flaws.

value of event (may be in error by an order of magnitude)	×	probability of event (at best dubious, at worst pure guess)

equals: list of decision base values
(which has high risk of being
incomplete or overlooking a significant vulnerability)

An Alternative: Using Information Valuation as a Guide

For years business has used physical security programs based on good police practices. People who have tried to justify a guard on a gate based on risk analysis have quickly found that it does not work. This is so because the incidence of physical penetration or damage is insufficient to build a case for justifying specific expenditures (e.g., why should we have a guard on the east gate— no troublemaker ever entered *there*!).

Security has been a concern of mankind since cave-dweller times. Reasonable management takes steps to protect assets. Business owners demand such steps, for reasons obvious and common. Medieval kings built moats and fortresses and used spies to protect against overt attack and covert threats. Analysis was not required—experience and common knowledge were sufficient.

Modern business does the same in many instances, providing locking facility doors, guards, fences, remote scan television monitors, and other systems that recognize the facts of a world that is not benign. These protective measures are considered "reasonable and justified," based on a perception of the operating environment. This perception is the result of actual experience, the news media, discussions, and the application of professional knowledge from the security managers.

A similar process can be used to develop, tailor, and justify investment in the protection of computer-processed information. The information values (or classifications) are used to determine the protective elements required at various stages of information processing (including human processing). A well-designed program, based on information values across the total processing environments is equally effective, and much more economical to implement than is a total program based on risk analysis methods. Security, like other business decisions, involves risk-taking. Within the established policy framework, division or unit managements continually evaluate risk versus security costs. Figure 8.2 illustrates the curves associated with achieving various levels of security for digital information. (These curves are not mathematically accurate but are merely illustrative.)

An information security protection cover presenting an extremely high work factor, or level of protection, will have an equivalently high cost in terms of administrative or procedural difficulty. As increasing numbers of would-be penetrators are shut out, the security mechanism also will deny entry to some number of authorized employees. An example will demonstrate the point.

Assume that a data file, maintained on a magnetic disk device on-line to a terminal, has a password protection. The password is five positives long and in fact is the name of the primary user of the file, "Nancy." Everyone in the department wishing to use the file may easily recall the password. And does. A penetrator, however, who has even rudimentary information about the business will know that Nancy is the primary system user and will start off any penetration attempt by trying names associated with the primary user. Husband's, mother's, son's, and daughter's names are all good bets for discovery of a simple password. So, although the authorized employees find "Nancy" convenient, so will a reasonably clever penetrator! Today's "hackers" can run through an entire dictionary in a matter of minutes. Hence any dictionary word is a poor password choice.

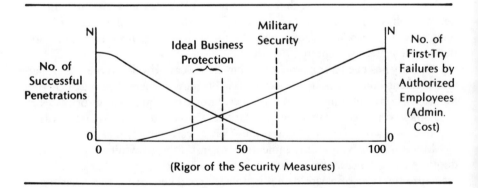

Figure 8.2   Relative penetration work factor (PWF) value versus cost.

Now let us assume that a program for electronic security is implemented and that the password is changed to a very rigorous form. The password now is eight positions in length and is randomly generated by the security subsystem. The password is now B933M12L, and the penetrator faces an almost-impossible task. But employees must continually call in the security officer, since they repeatedly forget or enter the wrong password. This administrative cost may be more than justified by the additional security provided.

Security benefits, especially in the office environment, are extremely difficult to quantify. Management and the security staff must be continually aware of the necessary tradeoffs, in terms of business operating requirements. Unrealistic security measures will be negated by the employees. In the example above, the employees would eventually write the password on pieces of paper, to be taped to terminal or wall. The security effect is then null.

Using information security management techniques as a basis for initiating a program of electronic information security has an important secondary benefit missing from the risk analysis method. That is, information must be protected in *all* forms, whether in computers, on paper, or passed by word of mouth. The total information security program should provide consistently effective protection across all forms.

A study of most so-called "computer crime" reveals that almost all cases begin with an exposure of information through paper—plain administrative carelessness. Locking up the computing systems without safeguarding the paper-borne information misses the point of computer security. The security effort must be a part of an overall information security program. After all, fraud occurred long before computers came on the scene.

A detailed risk analysis is supposed to provide management with data upon which to base security spending decisions. This is fairly reliable when the area surveyed is manageable, such as a single application at a branch office. Unfortunately, as the scope of the risk analysis increases, the quality of the product becomes even more dubious. The sparse supporting information and the analytic means available mean that decisions will be based on a large dose of "guesstimation," while exposures may be overlooked. Detailed risk analysis may provide management with a "security blanket" concerning spending and program thrust. Whether the cost of the analysis, which is significant if done properly, justifies this warm feeling remains to be seen. The security provided compared with that provided by using information valuation, in my opinion, does not justify the cost of formal analysis.

Risks are constantly shifting and changing in relation to technology developments. The use of judgment by skilled security people is the basis for both kinds of security program definition. Formal analysis generates the cost-risk tradeoff data (of more or less dubious parentage) beloved of financial analysts. Management should choose the method that results in the greatest comfort—the results will probably be the same.

WORKING THE PROGRAM

At this point it may be well to review the activities that have established the program for electronic information security. In sequence, these activities are

1. Publication of policy. This action establishes corporate management's intent to commit continuing resources to the safeguarding of business information wherever it occurs.
2. A network of security coordinators in the operating divisions or units is established for both implementation and maintenance purposes.
3. Standards are developed and published. The security coordinators jointly develop and publish standards that will provide detailed requirements to support the policy intent. Standards are the references for the division or unit business managers. Local procedure, if necessary, is developed from the standards.
4. Requirements survey. This detailed survey, against the established standards, provides input for business planning. The requirements survey identifies the actions, resources, and spending needed to achieve compliance over time. Typically, this time span may be two to three years.
5. Unit plan. This plan commits unit or division management to achieving compliance with policy and standards. The unit plan sets resource and spending levels and establishes milestones for completion of tasks leading to a level of security commensurate with the standards.

Ongoing program management will require some means for monitoring and evaluating unit performance against plans. This sixth activity, called key indicator reporting, allows unit and corporate managements to observe unit performance against the plans and to "take the pulse" of the program effort on a periodic basis. Table 8.1 illustrates the six activities in implementing a program for electronic information security.

Program Cycle

The working program for electronic information security has an orderly, cyclical flow of events, beginning with the inital recognition and commitment by top management expressed in a policy statement. The cycle of events, some of which repeat at a fairly regular timing, allows the program to regenerate and remain current with technology application.

The program activities are driven by business requirements, which may also be the prime driver for new applications of information technology. The program then also stays reasonably effective in consonance with business needs. This is most important. The information security program must be suited to business requirements. Regular reviews and replanning activities help ensure currency and appropriateness to the business environment, which in a big company is always changing.

Table 8.1 Program Activities in Sequence

Sequence	Activity	Description	Continuity
1	Policy publication	Management decision to commit to program for digital information security	One-time. Policy revision as needed (five to ten years)
2	Program organization	Appointment of security manager and unit security coordinators	Permanent appointments
3	Standards publication	Joint development and publication of detailed requirements for achieving information security	Reissue on a two-to-three year cycle, or as required, based on technology applications
4	Requirements survey	Detailed survey at unit level to identify actions required to meet policy	Should be reviewed whenever there is a change in environment, equipment, or a change in policy
5	Unit plan publication	Unit-developed multiyear plan for resources, spending, and compliance activity to meet standards requirements	Annual review and reissue. Basis for key indicator reporting
6	Key indicator reporting	Quarterly or other periodic reporting against unit plan	Quarterly review by unit management and corporate staff. Annual review by corporate management

A large company, with sales of $1 billion or more annually, probably has a program cycle of about three years, during which the company

- Performs requirements survey
- Reviews standards against business needs
- Reevaluates (by survey if appropriate) situation
- Regenerates requirements through new standard (or policy)
- Obtains recommitment and support

Plans are based on the inital requirements survey, which measures current situations against the standards. Plans will probably extend over several years, although annual reissuance of the plan is in most cases appropriate to mesh with business planning and funding cycles. Unit business plans should include resource needs for electronic as well as other kinds of security. Electronic security plans resulting from the security requirements survey provide the targets and schedules of accomplishment that should move the unit or division toward full compliance with policy. Compliance with policy is achieved when the unit substantially meets all the minimum protection levels established in the standards. In cyclical fashion, each unit's business plan should build on the previous year's accomplishments, moving the unit toward complete satisfaction of the work items identified in the requirements survey.

Eventually, probably about three years after initial program start, some units may wish to review the situation of requirements, spending, and achievements. Another requirements survey, or a lesser security review, would be appropriate for this purpose. About every two or three years, or as changes occur that affect business methods or technology applications, both policy and standards should be reviewed for currency. Today's rate of change and increasing use of computing make such reviews absolutely necessary if the electronic information security program is to be effective. Figure 8.3 illustrates the program cycle, which will be different in cycle times and content for each business situation.

Reporting and Key Indicators

Regular evaluation of program progress, against established requirements, is accomplished through the reporting procedures. Evaluation of the effectiveness of applied security elements, as standards compliance is achieved, is another matter. This is a case of judgment, test, and analysis by competent technicians by security reviews or requirements surveys.

Corporate security staff should collect and assemble, for summarization for top management, data concerning "key indicators," which will provide information indicating the extent to which each unit or division is meeting plan requirements. It is well to accept that perfect security is never achievable. Rather, security must be viewed as a continuum, with no security at one end and perfect security at the other. Although perfect security is never reached, the goal is continuing progress along the continuum in that direction.

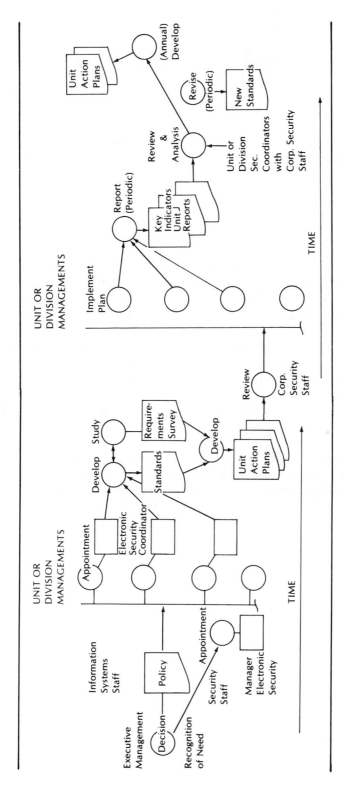

Figure 8.3 Electronic information security program; program cycle and information flow.

127

The plan should provide such impetus. The key indicators should be selected to indicate to the security manager, and ultimately to top management, that orderly progress is being made at a satisfactory rate, that is, per the plan. The key indicators have four functions:

1. They simplify reporting requirements for the units.
2. They simplify the task of the security staffs at all levels in evaluating progress against plan.
3. They indicate the important items versus the trivial.
4. They should allow cross-information about the progress of solutions aimed at common problems.

The security coordinator at each division or unit is the responsible action officer for ensuring that plan schedules are accomplished. Although unit or division line management is ultimately responsible for security (this must have been established when initial policy was written), the security coordinator provides the managerial impetus to the program. The security coordinator does this by

- Working with line management to ensure that appropriate funds are included in the unit budget according to the plan
- Tracking progress against the plan and reporting this to unit or division management
- Reporting on key indicators to the unit management and to the corporate manager of electronic security

The prime purpose for the security coordinator at each unit is cross-fertilization and the assignment of single points to resolve common problems. The key indicators should provide a means for monitoring results and sharing benefits.

Examples of key indicators are given in Table 8.2. The corporate manager of electronic security should develop those which best fit the program and plan requirements, along with any special interest items from top management.

Table 8.2 indicates that some activities have continuity; that is, they are more than one-time efforts. The key indicators established to monitor unit activity and progress initiate cyclical renewal of policy and standards. Unit security coordinators may identify new requirements or may find that already recognized security problems have novel characteristics requiring development of new security elements. Instances such as these should trigger an effort to revise or replace standards and, on a much longer-term basis, may lead to rewriting of policy.

Table 8.2 Suggested Key Indicators

Is year-to-date electronic information security spending according to plan?
Are all value-factor files and systems protected by access management systems?
Is a formal security program established with specific assignments of responsibilities?
Are special interest development items proceeding according to agreed schedules?

Information Flow

The flow of information in the following areas depends on the management relationships set up by the program:

- Requirements (standards) currency and acceptability
- Newly recognized vulnerabilities
- New or revised standards
- Problems and progress
- Unit-developed procedure or method

The security manager and the unit security coordinators together form a network to transmit information and assistance. The network also has a collective responsibility to develop good standards. Line management direction flows from corporate management through the standards to unit or division management. In terms of directives, the security manager and the network are staff adjuncts, implementors, and reporters. Management operates and evaluates the program through the network.

Line Responsibility for Information Security

Functional users or originators of information are regarded as "data owners" for security purposes. To achieve full participation and, hence, effective security application by these information users, units may wish to set up management security councils. One appropriate reason for setting up a management review council or board in a large operating unit is to provide insight into new program directions. Information processing technology is among the prime driving forces for changes in the way business operates. As such, technology applications or intrusions into business practices almost always carry security implications. Were it possible to predict future requirements, an ongoing cyclical program would not be necessary. With technology development at its present rate, and projected to provide even more innovation in the near term, a unit information security review committee can help to keep the program effectively in perspective with business needs and methods. Members could include systems managers and functional managers, with a security coordinator or manager as recorder. Examples of situations where a management review committee fills a need are easily provided:

A personnel department wishes to have access to information currently in data files. A separate database is set up, fed from the central files, and provided with inquiry capabilities. Who is allowed access, and under what circumstances? How will access controls be established and maintained? Are there various levels of access by job, salary, accessor responsibility, etc.? A review committee can assist in clarifying administrative positions that are essential to gaining control and ensuring security for the information files.

A communicating word processing and administrative services system is installed in executive offices. Who should have access? How will accessors be controlled? Are there to be limits on the data stored or processed on the system? The management panel can get answers to these questions and assist the security coordinator in implementing effective protection systems.

This need should not be confused with formal risk evaluation. The security elements must be good enough to determine that risks and vulnerabilities are sufficiently offset. "Sufficiently" may be synonymous with "reasonably," since the security of computer-processed information must be provided for in a manner that harmonizes with overall business goals. The determination of what is "sufficient," or in harmony, is a continuing process. Inputs to the program cycle, in the form of recommendations from operating units, should flow through the unit or division security coordinators to the corporate level.

In the early years of program operation, comments will usually address additional coverages required. In later times people will begin to see overlapping coverages, redundancies, improved methods, and new technology, which will allow some requirements to be set aside or replaced.

Continuing Program Development

It is said that one never stands still but either advances or slides back. A good program must have a continuing interchange of methods or ideas. The reader should not, in any case, consider the policy, standards, and security methods presented herein as gospel. Each business has its own characteristics and security requirements. Especially in the fast-developing application of distributed or "personal" computing, security requirements must be constantly developed and tailored to business needs.

To those ends, the program should offer some regular opportunities for key program participants to exchange ideas and to learn about new methods from peers or experts. The idea of a "network" of security coordinators has already been mentioned. This group of knowledgeable people, from each division or unit, constitutes the most valuable resource in terms of contribution to program content and effectiveness. Some ideas on program development are listed below, especially where the business organization is a large one:

1. The corporate manager of electronic security could publish a regular newsletter on electronic security, providing ideas from the technical security literature, from peers at other companies, and from correspondents and, most important, telling what the operating units or divisions are doing. This could include plans, difficulties, and accomplishments.
2. Regular meetings of the division security coordinators, perhaps on a regional basis to conserve travel costs, could be held where these people could exchange ideas and contribute to mutual growth.
3. The corporation could sponsor a regular (annual?) electronic information security conference, with invited speakers on subjects of current interest to

the business. Often, computer vendors are happy to gain the exposure and can provide very capable technologists.

4. The corporate security director or staff should make periodic staff visits to the operating divisions. In some cases this may be for purposes of formal program status review but at other times merely for a "hello" visit, perhaps with a helpful presentation on new program ideas or concerns.

A continual, information-rich exchange of ideas, needs, and solutions is an ingredient of a successful program. The many workshops, meetings, seminars, and conferences held by professional groups are excellent sources.

Training

The security coordinator is responsible for the training and currency of division personnel in the requirements of the security program. The standards are the basis for the training effort. For most companies, a formal training program, with copies of the materials being provided to each security coordinator, will be most economical and satisfactory in the long run. The goal is to achieve a common level of understanding and awareness throughout the company. Every employee using or processing digital information should have training.

A program based on announcements and the publication of materials will not succeed. Each employee must be indoctrinated with the importance of the security program. In the technical community, responsibilities for electronic information are greater, and training is especially important where people have personal computing capabilities. A good information security program will provide

1. Training materials suitable to all audiences (Figure 8.4)
2. Security awareness modules for inclusion in company technical training efforts
3. Pamphlets, handouts, and similar awareness builders
4. Periodic special security seminars (perhaps with the aid of computer manufacturers)
5. A regular newsletter or similar device for those directly involved in computer security.

Security Reviews

Management support, expressed through the commitment of resources, is the key to an effective electronic information security program. Unit or division managers, through the security coordinator, establish and maintain the required efforts. Periodic review of the unit or division security program is a good idea, however, because such a review provides a fresh view of the situation, helps create a cooperative effort among divisions and corporate headquarters, may identify problems that need to be addressed, may indicate the need for revision of electronic information security standards, and gives corporate management current information on the effectiveness and currency of division programs.

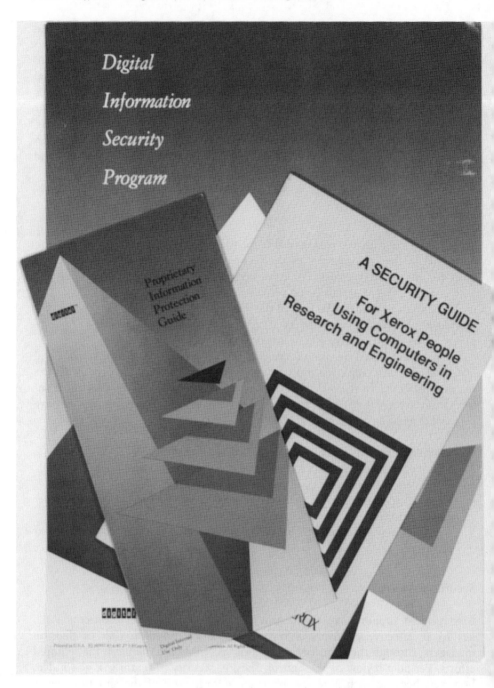

Figure 8.4   Training materials.

A security review is not an audit. Auditing (see the following section) is a separate function that addresses the question of effective management control. A security review is a cooperative effort between corporate security staff and unit or division management and their security coordinators. The basis for a security review should be a checklist developed from the Electronic Information Security Standards. Such a checklist may be similar (although never the same) to the checklist used by the company auditors. Each important requirement from the standards should be rephrased as a question, preferably answerable by yes or no or satisfactory or unsatisfactory. The checklist should provide references to the standards with each question. Appendix 5 shows a checklist used for security review.

Since an electronic information security review is a cooperative effort, unit or division management must agree to, or ask for, such a review. Representatives of the corporate security manager and the unit security coordinator conduct the review. Unit management is given the opportunity to comment on the written report of the security review before it is finalized. The agreed report should then be the basis for such action commitments as are appropriate. Actions required should become a part of a cyclical information security management process.

Keep in mind that the review should never be used as a basis for management criticism or punishment. It is a cooperative, constructive effort to understand the status of the information security program in the unit or division, and to develop suggestions for program improvement. Perfect information security is impossible to achieve. Do not be surprised or upset when deficiencies are noted in such a review. The goal is to continue to improve security in line with established policy requirements.

Auditing

Although the network of security coordinators described earlier is the implementing means for a program for computer-processed information security, an enforcement mechanism is needed. People will do what they are supposed to do, and do it better, when someone is "checking up" on them.

The company auditors, or internal auditors, are the best enforcement means. Although security and audit purposes do not always coincide, one overriding common purpose makes them good working partners. That purpose is the protection and conservation of company resources. Four major benefits accrue from using the internal auditors to review security program compliance:

1. The auditors have an authoritative position that transcends local or division management.
2. Auditors are free from political entanglements, which may make difficulties for security staff.
3. Regular audits are scheduled for critical functions, thus giving management and security staff a chance for an objective review of the security effort.

4. Exchange of information between the audit staff and the security staff provides opportunities for general discussions of risks and concerns.

The security manager should establish working relationships with internal auditors and should prepare an audit checklist for their use. They will probably revise the checklist to fit in with the particular audit style used in the company, but the input from the security manager will ensure that audits take security concerns into account in each assignment and address the particular issues.

Computer-trained auditors are a necessity if such a liaison is to pay off. Suitable auditing software packages should be available. Auditors should go to their work equipped with the latest version of company security standards and an understanding of the import of those standards. The security manager has a role to play in indoctrination of auditors on the intent and procedures of the company program for computer-processed information security.

Audit reports should always include a security module, one that addresses the security requirements for the particular function being audited. When computer systems or computing devices are in use at the audited function, the auditors should always comment whether the applicable standards are being followed.

The security manager should be provided a confidential copy of all draft audit reports. Comments on the audit work results can then be made to the audit coordinator or other official, who can see that proper corrective action is directed as part of the ongoing audit process.

An important side benefit from having auditors review security program compliance is that the security staff members remain insulated from an "inspection and audit" activity. This means that security "reviews" can be conducted with the full cooperation of division or regional staffs, in the knowledge that forthcoming reports will be recommendations and not directives. The cooperation and openness needed to ensure a good security program will not be compromised by fear of unfavorable reverberations through the lines of authority.

Contingency Preparation

In my view, contingency planning is a separate subject that addresses management's responsibility for broad planning for cases where protective systems fail or are overcome by nature or events. Because a limited contingency planning activity is usually associated with electronic information security, the subject will be discussed briefly.

Contingency planning cannot be done effectively if it is limited to a portion of the business. Making contingency plans for data processing while ignoring potential disasters in other, equally important parts of the business is irresponsible. For one thing, distributed personal computing is moving the computer resource out into the organization, where the computing elements will be dispersed. A loss of a major office building could result in the loss of a significant computing resource, totally outside the data center.

The loss of a key manufacturing facility or the loss of a source of critical parts or supplies could be as crucial, or perhaps more so, to continued business operation as the loss of a data center, depending on the business.

Contingency planning is too important to be left to the information systems and security people. It must be addressed as a major corporate issue, on an all-encompassing basis. Security and information systems managers have a role to play, but it must be within an overall business requirements framework to be effective.

All businesses should maintain complementary programs of insurance and disaster planning. As in the case of a personal insurance program, coverage should be limited to those risks the business is unwilling to bear. An outline of a contingency program might include

1. Loss of business insurance—deductible policy.
2. Recovery and alternative processing plans for those few information systems essential to the continued viability of the business, e.g., billing and receivables, payroll. It is doubtful if any large company can reasonably plan replacement of its system or network in total.
3. Recovery and alternatives planning for any key production elements, e.g., parts manufacturing.

Good security and safety planning and implementations should help avoid situations where the contingency plan must come into play. But note that contingency planning is a separate issue. Security programs, including that for electronic information security, are part of the management responsibilities for ongoing business operation. Contingency planning, on the other hand, is concerned with the possibility that ongoing operations may be halted because of circumstances beyond management control.

Contingency planning is strategic; security planning is tactical. Contingency planning must therefore be done at the highest levels and may involve decisions concerning elimination of major portions of the business or its assets. The contingency planning process might include

- Determining key activities for business continuity. These are the major production, marketing, and administrative functions that must, at any cost, be maintained if the business is to survive. This decision must be made by the CEO or by a committee appointed by the CEO.
- Identifying the resources involved in those key activities. Some of those resources will undoubtedly be information systems.
- Developing recovery and alternative operation plans for those resources supporting the key activities.
- Rehearsing to the extent practicable, the implementation of the contingency operation, at least in simulated form. Be as realistic as possible, and keep scrupulous notes of activities and problems.
- Continuing to refine and improve contingency planning.

If thorough planning is difficult in the usual business environment, it will be even more difficult after the catastrophe has happened. The most difficult step is the first one. Each functional executive wants to see his activity as important to the business, but the company cannot plan to recover from every possibility. That is why the business insurance is provided. Only the very few, truly essential elements can be protected through contingency planning.

THE FUTURE

Rapid developments in computing hardware technology will continue to drive business, especially large ones, to automate functions previously performed manually.

- Hardware technology will provide smaller and more economical computing elements, almost as a reducing logarithmic function (cost and size reduced by 50 percent annually).
- Automation of functions will increase as the increasing cost of labor and decreasing cost of computing power provide a powerful economic driver.
- Computers, and workstations designed to fit business needs, are changing the information patterns in business operations. The security vulnerabilities are also changing as access and processing move away from traditional centers and into homes, airports, automobiles, airplanes, and even suppliers' and contractors' premises.
- Computing power will continue to increase spectacularly as instructions processed per second (MIPS) double with the introduction of each new technology.

From a security view, this implementation of computing systems in all phases of business operations implies greater movement of information in electronic form and, as a result, greater vulnerability to clandestine, unauthorized access. Exposure to fraud is most severe where information mode (such as physical, on paper, and electronic, as in a computer) changes, usually involving human intervention. These mode changes are most common, and the vulnerability of the information most serious, around the "pockets" of automation. These pockets will occur in the process of converting office or administrative systems to automated methods.

For example, a group of executive secretaries in a division headquarters may be provided with information processing systems that can handle text processing, communications, filing, "electronic mail," and graphics. Other secretaries in that division, however, and secretaries in other parts of the corporation may not have such equipment. The secretaries using the computer systems must then receive some information in paper form and must convert it to electronic form for the electronic mail and file system. Conversely, they will have to print out memos and letters, either locally or at remote stations, for delivery to those secretaries not having computer communications. This conversion process is a danger point.

Whenever information exists in two forms at one time, there is increased risk. Additionally, as new systems are installed and new pockets of automation are created, there are temporary risks in each case until the old methods are phased out. These risks result from three factors:

1. The learning curve in coping with new requirements
2. A tendency to revert to old methods if difficulties arise, therein possibly skipping security requirements
3. The human tendency to have "backup" duplicates, just in case a new method does not work so well

The prognostications for the continued deliveries of more advanced, faster information processing and communications services at the personal and organizational levels mean that the cyclical program regeneration process will be essential. This process, wherein policy and standards are renewed on a cyclical basis, is the only way to keep the electronic information security program abreast of technology. An effective program for electronic information security is not a luxury, but a necessity.

Epilogue

The program described in this book has now been in use in a major corporation, with a few minor changes, for more than ten years. As with any complex, dynamic situation, it is difficult to analyze results in an objective manner.

The program has not prevented certain information-related incidents, but these have been relatively few. Management considers the investment in the program to be a wise use of resources.

By working the program, we have discovered the flaws and vulnerabilities, or at least most of these, in the system. The security coordinator concept, where used consistently, has resulted in an employee population well seeded with people who are aware of security requirements and are motivated about security. The senior computer security people have formed a committee, whose purpose is to review and republish standards (about every three years now), and to select and install technology as appropriate. A recent project saw the companywide installation of a PC security package.

Extensive use of a company *Internet* of local area networks has led to the automation of almost all security functions. For example, any employee, worldwide, can access a file of security policies and standards from his or her workstation. Periodic security letters are distributed electronically. Electronic mail is used regularly to comunicate security information.

Finally, the division between "security professionals" and computer security specialists is rapidly disappearing. The computer has become an essential part of our information lives.

APPENDIX 1

An Information Security Policy

SUMMARY

Protection of valuable or sensitive business information is critical to the company's continued successful and profitable business operations.

Certain business and technical information, because of its sensitivity, is classified as *company registered, company private,* or *company personal* and is to be marked accordingly. This information is to be protected at all times and in all forms (on paper, in electronic computer form, and in mental form in the minds of employees). Access to or knowledge of such information is based on need to know, following from assigned job tasks. Protection measures include avoiding careless talk, maintaining a clean desk, control over disclosure to outside parties, and avoiding unnecessary distribution internally. Public disclosure of information to the press, release of financial information, and comments on legal affairs are subject to limitations specified herein.

Technical and new product information is subject to specific limitations, the most significant of which is prior approval for release.

The security of electronic information, because of its unique operational characteristics and inherent security risks, is subject to additional security provisions. Some are addressed here, and others are addressed in greater detail in the company's information security standards (page 147).

This policy sets out the specific responsibilities of the company information executive, company security, operating groups, managers, employees, and security coordinators. Detailed information is provided in the company's information security standards, which are issued separately.

SCOPE

All Company operations.

POLICY

All units of the company will install adequate safeguards to protect the following information:

- Proprietary business and technical information
- Personal data concerning applicants, employees, and former employees
- Proprietary information of suppliers provided under contractual agreement

Classification

The company's internal classification system identifies valuable information and indicates which measures in a set of established, uniform practices are to be applied to protect sensitive business and technical information. The classifications are

- *Company Registered*—that information, the unauthorized disclosure of which could cause serious damage to company operation. This is the highest company classification. Its use, and the access to information so classified, must be strictly limited.
- *Company Private*—information of such value or sensitivity that its unauthorized disclosure could have a substantially detrimental effect on company operation.
- *Company Personal*—that information of a descriptive, personal nature that (1) a reasonable individual determines might be limited in its disclosure or that (2) an originator determines should be limited in its disclosure.

Information owners (usually the senior functional manager responsible) and, when necessary, originators of information are responsible for assigning appropriate company classification. The general counsel is the ultimate authority with regard to classification of all product-related technical material. Declassification takes place in accordance with schedules and procedures defined in the information security standards (also published in booklet form).

Handling and Marking

Company classified information in documents, electronic form, or both is to be marked, distributed, copied, mailed, hand carried off premises, stored, and destroyed only in accordance with prescribed company standards, which are specified in the information security standards.

PROTECTION OF INFORMATION

Awareness

Programs will be implemented to ensure that all employees are advised of their responsibility for protecting company classified information and the reasons therefore. All employees will read and sign the "proprietary information and conflict of interest agreement" during initial employment processing. The signed original form is retained in the employee's personnel file.

Careless Talk

Unnecessary or careless talk about company information, plans, strategies, unannounced products, research developments relating to products, and so forth must be avoided both at and away from the job. Under no circumstances should there be any discussion with outsiders of prospective growth, sales, earnings, research efforts, new products, contract awards, acquisitions and divestitures of business or properties, law suits, unannounced changes in management personnel, or other unpublished company information.

Clean Desk

All company employees must adhere to the "clean desk" policy. During non-business hours or when a workplace is unattended for more than two hours, all business information, classified or not, must be adequately secured. Adherence to the clean desk policy and the handling of classified information must be in accordance with the information security standards.

Dissemination of Information Within the Company

"Need to know" is a self-imposed discipline on the dissemination of all business information, whether classified or not. At the heart of this discipline is the determination by the originator or receiver that the information is of value to the user and is needed by the user to carry out his or her function. The number of people to whom such information is distributed must be strictly limited.

Disclosure of Information to Outside Parties

If, in the course of business, consultants, contractors, and other outside parties must have access to company classified material, they must sign a "confidential disclosure agreement." They are to receive only such information as is necessary to comply with their contract and must conform to company information-handling procedures. A master for the form is located in the information security standards.

Publications

Company publications intended for wide distribution to employees (e.g., telephone directories, newsletters) will contain only nonsensitive information. Although publication of scholarly or research material is permitted after required clearances have been obtained, company proprietary information must not be compromised.

PUBLIC DISCLOSURE OF INFORMATION

Press Relations

The company's public relations department is solely responsible for dealings with the press. The significance of information to be released must be carefully assessed by the originators beforehand. In virtually every case, clearance by the general counsel is required.

Release of Financial Information

Financial information—other than published financial statements, SEC statements, and sundry data previously made public by authorized company officials—is confidential information and may not be released to outside agencies, individuals, and foreign subsidiaries unless such release is approved by the CFO, comptroller, or treasurer or their designees.

Included under this definition is all data normally contained in company financial statements and notes as well as related statistical information such as products sold, supplies sold, line of business reporting, forecast of results of operations, budgets, plans, and so forth.

Legal Affairs

Any inquiries with respect to the company's legal affairs should be referred promptly to the general counsel. Legal affairs such as proposed or ongoing litigation; proceedings before governmental agencies; inquiries or investigations by federal, state, or local government; subpoenas or demands to produce company documents or other information; and contractual controversies with others can be highly sensitive and therefore must not be discussed outside the company.

Speeches and Publications

Wherever the author of any speech, article, presentation, or statement, or participant in a panel discussion, outside education program, or other activity intended for public release, is to be identified with the company, or if the content mentions the company or discusses any company matters whatsoever, the following clearance must be obtained before publication, delivery, or participation.

- For nontechnical material, clearance must normally be granted by a department manager, general counsel, and the cognizant manager of public relations.
- For technical material or material that refers to current or future products, research plans, or programs, additional approvals are required from general counsel.

Employment advertising for forward technical areas, technical training programs for customers, discussions of technical data with job applicants, organization announcements of components involved in advanced technology, new product development and other sensitive projects, and participation in trade shows and trade association meetings are all subject to prior approval requirements.

ELECTRONIC INFORMATION SECURITY

The unique operational characteristics and inherent security risks of electronic forms of information make it essential that special security programs be implemented for these systems. These provisions are specified in the company's information security standards.

RESPONSIBILITIES

Information Executive

- Develop and revise policies and procedures for safeguarding information
- Prepare training programs as required
- Ensure implementation of programs
- Provide guidance and leadership in resolving information management problems
- Ensure the establishment of a security coordinator network in operating units
- Perform staff visits and reviews as necessary
- Ensure internal auditing of operating units for conformance to information policies and procedures

Operating Groups

- Develop an organization to implement information management policy
- Develop, publish, and implement information control plans to achieve adherence to policy

- Initiate policies, standards, and procedures that are necessary for local requirements and legislation
- Obtain review and concurrence of information management implementation plans by the company information executive
- Conduct operating unit compliance reviews
- Identify and correct problem situations
- Report significant information security breaches and compromises to the company information executive

Managers and Employees

- Ensure adherence to policy and related procedures
- Protect company classified material in accordance with established policies and procedures
- Ensure that security indoctrination is provided to employees and contract and temporary personnel assigned to the organization
- Designate security coordinators as required
- Monitor implementation of information security regulations and programs

Security Coordinators

- Be fully conversant with security policies and guidelines
- Provide counsel to their management on security matters
- Carry out tasks and programs as set forth in the security coordinator guide and perform special assignments as required

APPENDIX   2

Information Security Standards

PREFACE

All employees are responsible for protecting company information by

- Making timely information classification decisions
- Using appropriate security measures and diligent care, per these standards.

BACKGROUND

Quality business information has the characteristics of *reliability* (available when and where needed), *integrity* (complete, accurate, free from unauthorized change), and *privacy* (not exposed to unauthorized parties). Security is an essential element, along with good systems design, supervision, and training, in providing quality information for company business purposes.

PURPOSE

These information security standards implement *company security policy*. They deal with protection of information in all forms. The standards provide detailed guidance to all employees using information systems of all types (including manual information systems and voice message systems).

ORGANIZATION

For convenience, the standards are arranged by subject, as follows:

Title   *Current date Page*

General Requirements

Outside Service and Connections

Application Development and Implementation

Information Processing and Telecommunications

Personal, Office, and Distributed Computing

Exceptions to Policy

References
   Company *Information Handling Regulations*
   Company information security policy

For assistance, ask your unit security manager, local security coordinator, or corporate security.

General Requirements

Objective

To specify the generally applicable *electronic security* elements to be used whenever company information is in electronic form.

Scope

These electronic security standards apply to all organizations worldwide. Employees managing or using information systems (including but not limited to manual information handling, word processors, workstations, intelligent copiers, computer terminals, network devices, network printers, and CAD/CAM/CAE systems) are responsible for understanding and compliance.

Exceptions

Where valid business reasons indicate alternative protection methods, the exception process applies.

Default

Should a mix of company classifications or a combination of circumstances create doubt about which requirement applies, the most rigorous security protection method will be used.

Definitions*

Prime User.   The manager responsible for the information processed (the data owner). This is usually the senior functional manager responsible for an activity or application that is the principle user of the information element or the manger responsible for budgeting for or controlling the information system.

User.   The end user or system user, for example, the employee using a system or device such as a terminal, minicomputer, microcomputer, word processor, electronic typewriter, telecopier, personal workstation, or CAD/CAM/CAE device.

Security coordinator.   An employee assigned an additional responsibility to serve as the local expert on security matters. He or she ensures general awareness and compliance with these standards by following the security coordinators' guide and by providing assistance to managers and employees as needed.

Exception to Policy.   An approval at a senior management level of a decision to use alternative protection measures or to accept unusual risks for business purposes.

Electronic Security Levels.   The classes or types of protective measures (e.g., physical, procedural, and logical). Within each level are electronic security elements, access management controls, and clean desk policy.

Electronic Security Elements.   The basic building blocks for constructing protective barriers such as

- *Physical elements:* door locks, guards, closed circuit television monitors, trespass alarms, entry control systems, and shielding to minimize emanations
- *Procedural elements:* document markings, document and disk storage containers, records of employee authorizations to access information, password change histories, computer use logs, monitoring of records, inspection of systems software changes, controls over documentation changes, and separation of duties as appropriate
- *Logical elements:* software and hardware functions that control user activity, provide for identification, authentication, and authorization of users to access or process information, and allow encryption of information

Access Management Controls.   The process that applies procedural and logical *security elements* to ensure

- *Identification of users,* through the presentation of a unique personal token, for example, something the user has (plastic card), knows (password), or is (fingerprint, voice). Usually, identification tokens are codes (passwords,

---

*(Defined terms are italicized in the text of these standards.)

identification numbers, account numbers) that are individually assigned but are not necessarily secret.

- *Authentication* of claimed identity, through a secondary means of identification (one of the forms of tokens as described above) that is private to an individual and kept secret.
- *Authorization* to perform specified actions by match of an autheniticated user against a predefined set of access privileges.
- *Monitoring of system activities* through regular observation of system activity logs and records, especially exceptional items which appear to be abnormal.

Clean Desk.   The company practice that requires that all business information be removed from view or otherwise protected when the workplace is unoccupied for two hours or more. For systems *users,* this means taking action to place a terminal or microcomputer in an idle mode, returning magnetic media to secure storage locations, and otherwise ensuring that unauthorized parties cannot gain access to company business information.

Responsibilities

Employees (*users*) are responsible for protecting company information in all forms. Employees may not use information systems for purposes other than as authorized by the responsible manager.

Electronic security administrators and coordinators are responsible for assisting employees and managers to fulfill electronic security responsibilities and providing advice and expertise as necessary. Problems or incidents must be promptly reported to operating unit security.

Managers are responsible for controlling employee use of information systems. Effective controls include appropriate supervision; regular, periodic security reviews; analysis of computing spending reports; and application of *access management control* systems (see below).

Access Management Control Systems.   Devices connected to networks (directly or by dialup) or processing company classified information require the following controls:

1. A unique, personal *identification* token (e.g., employee identification, account code) must be assigned to each user.
2. A unique, personal *authentication* token (e.g., password, fingerprint) must be used to validate the identity claimed. Passwords must be kept secret. To be effective, passwords should have at least six characters and must be changed at least every 90 days for business and engineering (CAM, CAD, CAE) systems and every 180 days for scientific and research and development systems. System software or systems administration shall enforce such changes. *Authentication tokens* shall be stored in the system in encrypted form and must never be displayed in cleartext.

3. The system *authorization* process controls user activity by referring to a list of objects (files, records, data types, hardware devices, and programs) allowed and to a level of access (read-copy, update, create-delete, execute) as established by the *prime user.*

4. For company classified information, individual "need to know" access privileges must be established and the system must limit access and subsequent activity accordingly; for *business registered* information, the system also must provide user activity logs.

5. The system must suppress display of the *authentication token* and must limit unsuccessful attempts to sign-on to some reasonable number of tries (maximum ten). The system logs any such unsuccessful attempts. The log should be monitored. Continuous unsuccessful attempts at sign-on should result in suspension of account privileges pending investigation.

6. Administration controls must ensure that *access authorizations* are canceled or changed on employee job changes that modify need-to-know status, transfer, or termination. Such control usually involves cancellation of *user* accounts. This should be done through a formal mechanism, preferably tied to personnel procedures.

7. Company classified documents must be properly stored if to be left unattended for more than two hours. Access devices left unattended in active mode must be automatically shut off, returned to idle mode, or otherwise protected consistent with the *clean desk* policy.

8. If the system is to be used to process *business registered* information in unencrypted form, the hardware must be equipped to prevent interception of data from signal emanations.

Information Protection

Information classifications are assigned by the *prime user,* or by the *user* in situations where personal computing (including word processing) may generate new information. The information classifications and protection requirements are explained in detail in the *Information Handling Regulations* booklet available from *security coordinators,* security managers, or corporate security. Briefly, these requirements are as as follows:

- *Business registered,* the highest classification. This is information that, if disclosed, could cause serious damage to company operations. Encryption of *registered* information is required when transmitted over telecommunications circuits and when stored on non-removable magnetic media (removable media must be stored in a bar lock cabinet or a safe container meeting policy requirements). All security elements levels must be applied. Access is allowed only to specifically identified individuals.
- *Private data* is information that, if disclosed, could have a substantially detrimental effect on company operations.

- *Personal data* is information that, if disclosed, might be embarrasing or detrimental to an individual or to the company. For either *private data* or *personal data,* appropriate security elements must be applied to prevent unauthorized disclosure, modification, or destruction. Access is allowed only to those employees who have a "need to know."

All other information is for internal use only unless publicly announced or published.

The transfer of technical or personal data to persons or organizations outside the originating country may be controlled by government regulations and by contractual obligations. Criminal penalties often apply to violations. For details, see the appropriate data protection officer, export-import coordinatior, or legal counsel.

General marking and handling requirements are as follows:

- Company classified information must be protected from casual observation at all times. Classified information in written or visual display forms must be clearly marked with the appropriate security symbol, or computer-generated equivalent, large enough to be obvious. Documents must be protected at all times in process, storage, and delivery. For delivery of *business registered* documents, use certified mail or receipted express mail. Do not put classification markings on the outside package (except for *personal* data in specially marked envelopes). Degauss, erase, shred, or otherwise destroy company classified information on documents or magnetic media before scrapping or transfer to others. Fixed disks containing company classified information must be cleared of such data through initialization, reformatting, writing over, or similar means before transfer to others or when information is no longer required.
- When unattended output devices (e.g., facsimile devices, network printers) are used, special arrangements must be made to ensure that company classified information is fully protected from loss, copying, or unauthorized observation.

Outside Services and Connections

Objective

To ensure consistent protection of company information when processed in computers operated by other than the company; when noncompany-originated application software or services are used; and when company computers or networks are directly connected with such devices operated or controlled by other than the company.

Scope

All employees using outside computing, telecommunications or other services or approving external interconnections.

Definitions

Outside Services.   Any services involving electronic information processing or transfers provided by noncompany parties.

External Interconnections.   Any direct telecommunications connections established between company computer–network resources and outside parties–computing sources. This definition does not include the use of basic telephone or telecommunications services utilities (e.g., AT&T, British Telecom, Tymnet) for connections between company-operated computers or devices; it also does not include the use of general public services such as Dun & Bradstreet, travel reservations systems, or others that involve public services or one-way retrievals of information).

Requirements

Managers will take necessary actions to ensure continuing protection as follows:

1. *Business registered* information may not be processed by outside services nor transmitted by company-operated or by external interconnections including ARPANET, Telex, or other general communications utilities (e.g., AT&T, British Telecom, PTTs) unless encrypted.
2. Application software developed by outside parties may not be used to process *business registered* information unless approved on an exception basis. A list of such software, approved per the *exception process,* may be established by organizations processing *business registered* information regularly. Qualifying application software must meet all the other security requirements of these standards.
3. *Private data* and *personal data* may not be processed by outside services unless approved on an *exception basis.* Prudent care must be used when sending information in these classifications by Telex or other general communications utility that is not secure against casual observation.
4. Company network external interconnections are not permitted except for mail service through mail gateways. Any other connection requires an exception approval.
5. Outside access to other company networks or computing or office systems environments requires an exception approval. Persons or organizations authorized such access must be restricted to only that information required for accomplishing company-assigned tasks.
6. Where dialup connections to company computing resources involve access to company classified information, special controls must be applied. These may include (a) a software control package such as ACF-2, RAC-F, or similar, (b) use of a port protection device (callback), (c) encryption, (d) a manual procedure to identify callers, or (e) a combination of these elements appropriate to the classification assigned.
7. Connections with persons or systems in countries outside the originating country require special care to ensure compliance with national export con-

trol regulations, data transfer laws, and company contractual obligations. (For further information, see the export control coordinator, data security officer, or legal counsel.)

8. Systems processing company personal information must comply with national or other applicable privacy laws in all places to or from which data are transmitted.

Applications Development and Implementation

Objective

To ensure that applications are developed and implemented to provide consistent information protection appropriate to the company classification assigned.

Scope

All employees developing and implementing computing applications.

Requirements

Information systems organizations are responsible for assisting the *prime user, user,* or both in meeting requirements to protect company information.

Good systems design will ensure that consistent protection is provided throughout all system operations, including remote, distributed, and manual portions. This standard applies to all projects and individual development efforts; security must always be considered an essential requirement.

Project Initiation.   Identify extraordinary risks, especially those which could involve exposure of company classified information; write a statement of security requirements.

Project Definition.   The *prime user* makes a preliminary determination of company classification of the information to be processed. Caution: processing of multiple unclassified files may result in data combinations that should be classified.

Analysis and Planning.   Potential risks and exposures must be documented.

Design.   Controls must be developed that will bring attention to any attempts to perform unauthorized actions. Such controls must meet the requirements of data privacy legislation and must fix responsibility by providing audit trails. The system designer, acting in concert with the information security manager, will advise the *prime user* about the best security elements and methods, including access management control systems, administrative control of the granting of *user* authorizations, and encryption for *business registered* information. Database systems must be provided with logging, recovery, and function-penetration controls.

Procedure Development and Programming.   Good programming and procedure development practices are essential to security, as follows:

- Use simple, modular program construction to allow program verification.
- Testing must not use production data but must be done using test data or base case data developed for the purpose.
- Programs must be fully documented during the programming phase and before the installation report. Documentation must be stored securely according to the *Information Handling Regulations.*
- Systems must include controls and audit trails to allow tracking and verification of processing actions. If bulk data transfer from a PC is to be a part of the data input process, special procedures must be established to ensure auditability.
- Procedures must specify checks and balances, details of system *access management control* administration, contingency planning for restart and recovery procedures, and control of changes to the application environment (including programs, documentation, forms, and procedures).
- Before the system becomes operational, the *prime user* must be advised of any security requirements not met. If no resolution to meet these standards is possible before system implementation, an *exception approval* must be obtained.
- Procedures must be defined for emergency system changes to ensure adequate approvals before the fact or before changes become permanent. These approvals must include the *prime user* and the information security manager.

Information Processing and Telecommunications

Objective

To ensure that data processing centers and telecommunications operations organizations have enough security to ensure consistent protection for company information.

Scope

Applies to all organizations providing information processing and telecommunications services to a community of *prime users* and *users.*

Requirements

Managers of information processing and telecommunications service organizations are responsible for protecting information entrusted to their care for processing, transmission, or both in accordance with company classifications and the organization's implemented *electronic security elements.*

Information processing and telecommunications service organizations shall normally provide security at the level required for *private data.* To that end, a set of *security element* offerings shall be made available, including an *access management control* software package; *prime users* and *users* may select appropriate protection means from this set of security services. The security protections will be maintained consistently throughout networks and distributed systems and in accordance with applicable privacy legislation.

Environmental.   Positive *physical security elements* for access control will be established, both for entry to the general facility and for entry to more restrictive areas (e.g., operations, media library).

Input and Output.   Company information must be protected at all times whether in electronic or printed form. Outputs must be properly marked or stamped and delivered in a controlled manner (see above). Note that protected bulk delivery of company classified outputs can be provided by using receipted delivery services. Place a top sheet inside the sealed container with the classification indicated. The recipient signs for the contents and is responsible for further controlled distribution.

Operational.   Information processing and telecommunications service organizations must exercise positive control over operating system and hardware maintenance activities, processor loading and systems clock setting, and changes to operating documentation. An audit trail of all systems activities must be maintained and reviewed daily.

Magnetic Media.   Information processing and telecommunications service organizations must provide for secure storage, handling, and shipping of tapes, disks, cartridges, or other media. Release of any media must be strictly controlled based on company information security practices and "need to know" requirements for the various company classifications (see above). Shipments of media must be by courier, receipted delivery, or other secure means. Media must be securely packed with classification labels on the internal reel or disk, with the addressee only shown on the outside package. Periodic inventories of media are required to maintain effective control.

Personal Workstations and Office and Distributed Computing

Objective

To ensure that employees use the proper security measures to protect information processed on personal workstations, microcomputers, terminals, office systems, networks, and distributed systems.

Scope

This standard applies to all systems *users* doing company work on electronic information processing/communicating equipment, regardless of location.

Requirements

Employees.   Employees using personal workstations of all types including microcomputers, terminals, facsimile devices, communicating copiers, network-connected printers, electronic typewriters, and similar devices are responsible for protecting company information processed per *Information Handling Regulations*. Employes also must

- Maintain a secure, controlled workplace per the clean desk policy.
- Shield company classified information from casual view while on videodisplay terminal screen or desk; place electronic systems in idle mode when away from the workplace for more than two hours, or less as locally appropriate.
- Properly protect, mark, and store company classified outputs and magnetic media (tapes and disks).
- Apply suitable *access management controls* and use proper password discipline (see above).
- Ensure security of company classified documents produced on shared printing facilities (e.g., by network print servers).
- Use backup files as appropriate to ensure recovery from loss of data and continued effective business operations.

Electronic Security Coordinators. Electronic security coordinators ensure general awareness and compliance with these standards and provide advice and assistance to *users* as needed.

System Administrators.   System administrators for company networks are responsible for

- Ensuring proper security discipline on the part of network users by providing instructions for secure use of the network, file servers, and so on. The system administrator shall work closely with the security coordinator in this effort.
- Maintaining privacy of passwords and files entrusted to their care
- Encouraging proper *access management controls* including rigorous construction and protection of passwords by system users (see page 155)
- Ensuring proper physical security protection for file servers and communications servers
- Working with *users* to ensure proper document handling in cases where shared print facilities produce company classified information
- Providing backup files for information on file servers and general contingency planning to ensure continuity of business operations

Managers.   Managers are responsible for establishing effective controls over company information by

- Training employees in *Information Handling Regulations* procedures. Those employees with operational or technical duties (e.g., systems administrators, software and hardware maintenance specialists) must be made aware of their special security responsibilities.
- Controlling proper authorization to use electronic information processing and communicating equipment and by monitoring proper *access manage-*

ment control discipline, including ensuring that access privileges are properly cancelled on employee job change or separation

- Providing suitable physical and logical security *elements* for employee workplaces with special attention to general purpose computers or other information processors that may be situated in offices, plants, or other areas not designated as data centers
- Planning for contingency actions for recovery in event of disaster
- Establishing clear responsibility for systems-related actions, including *access management control,* and providing for separation of duties where sensitive responsibilities are to be met (e.g., systems software maintenance)
- Assigning *electronic security coordinator* responsibilities as appropriate and assigning security responsibilities to systems administrators as appropriate

Exceptions to Policy

Objective

To establish a procedure for management approval of decisions not to follow these standards. An *exception to policy* is an approval at a senior management level (defined below) of a decision to use alternative protection measures or to accept unusual risks justified by business requirements.

Scope

All managers responsible for the application or use of electronic information systems and communications.

Requirements

Managers.   Managers at all levels are responsible for ensuring continuing protection for company information as specified in these standards. When business requirements so dictate, company managers must obtain exception approval to use alternative protection methods or to accept unusual risks.

Procedure.   Exception to policy approvals must be obtained when

- Business requirements justify exceptions to these standards.
- Business requirements make a limited acceptance of risk appropriate.
- Unusual or severe risk is evident in a business proposal.
- Supplier premises are to be used for processing company classified information.
- Application-specific software developed outside the company is to be used for processing business registered information.
- Company network *external interconnections,* except for mail service through mail gateways, are implemented through approved products only. Any other connection requires an *exception* approval;

- *External interconnections* are to be established between company computers, devices, and telecom networks and noncompany computers, devices, and telecom networks.

Exception approval requests are processed as follows:

1. For *business registered* information, a written risk analysis must be provided. It should include the operating environment, a list of vulnerabilities and risks with probabilities assigned, potential results should an attack be successful, costs of such a successful attack, and a comparison of the cost of the alternative with the application of protection required per this standard. The exception request must be concurred in by the manager of corporate security and approved in writing by a group president, managing director, or corporate vice-president or equivalent.
2. For *private* or *personal* information, a written risk analysis must be provided. The exception request must be approved in writing by a division president, group vice-president, or corporate director or equivalent.
3. For all other company information, exception request must be approved in writing by a group vice-president or equivalent or a designee.

APPENDIX 3

Automated Logical Access Control*
Charles R. Symons
James A. Schweitzer

For most business data processed or communicated by computer, ensuring satisfactory security requires awkward compromises. Most business data are not sufficiently valuable that they need the sort of security measures that banks and the military typically employ to protect critical or private data. The intrinsic value of much financial or government information may make it worthwhile for a criminal to invest a large amount of money to steal a much larger sum or to obtain state secrets. Security measures therefore tend to be complex and thus expensive. For example, encryption is widely used to protect data in storage and transmission.

Most routine business data, however, do not warrant elaborate, expensive security protection. Indeed, security may be given a much lower priority than the goal of making the company's data easily accessible to large populations of users who need it for their jobs. As the costs of on-line working and office automation fall steadily compared with other costs, more and more employees are given direct access from personal workstations in their office or from home or other remote, physically insecure locations by dialup or direct connection to their data on business computers.

This same drive to improve accessibility, however, can also improve the chances of successful penetration of the computer system by unauthorized users. Basic business control reasons mean that some need-to-know restrictions on access are inevitably needed, even for authorized employees. Also, some categories of business data, such as personal data or commercially sensitive financial forecasts on product specifications, may require special security.

But business computers must also be secure against the attentions of people whose hobby is to try to "break-in," browse around, or trespass within computers. Recent frequent reports in the media indicate that this is a growing threat that must be taken seriously. Public concern has reached the point that the computer industry must respond to this threat.

---

*Adapted from Charles R. Symons and James A. Schweitzer, *Automated Logical Access Control* (Amsterdam: North Holland, 1982). Used with permission.

Summarizing the conflicting pressures on computer security, a typical business data processing or automated office community requires its computers and workstations to have a security system that

- Is reasonably priced consistent with business information values. Everyone wants the payroll kept secret, but no one wants to spend much to protect it.
- Offers minimal bureaucracy to the user community, which wants only to get at data.
- Requires only minimal effort by managers of the data processing service who do not want to have an expensive security administration or policing function; this suggests using the power of the computer itself to do the job.
- Is reasonably effective against the threats of carelessness, inquisitiveness, computer trespassing through networks, temptations to commit fraud, and so forth.

The security-cost-nuisance compromise that must be reached therefore lies somewhere between the "Fort Knox" and "Open House" extremes. A security barrier that is obviously going to require a significant effort to penetrate will deter most computer trespassers. It does not have to be a perfect barrier.

Computer security measures are normally considered under the headings of physical security, procedural security, and logical access security. The first two headings are well understood but are becoming relatively less important. When computers can be accessed from large numbers of remote terminals, users will be able to obtain business information without being physically present on the business premises or subject to procedural controls. Logical access security measures are those hardware and software processes that control access to data within computing systems for business control, privacy, and security purposes.

The purpose of this paper, therefore, is to examine the logical access security measures that a user, authorized or not, of a business data processing computer should encounter before he or she can start useful work. An optimum set of logical access controls is proposed, and, for reasons that will become apparent, a standard set of controls, automatically enforced by the computer, is recommended. The standard has been named automated logical access control standard (ALACS).

LOGICAL ACCESS CONTROL EFFECTIVENESS

Standard commercial logical access control software designed to protect business data normally puts three steps in the way of the user who wants to sign-on to the computer and perform certain tasks. These are

1. *Identification.* The user is required to enter a valid and uniquely identifying code, or "User ID." This could be, for example, a personnel number; it commonly doubles as an account code.

2. *Authentication.* Having been identified, the user is required to provide some code or token that is privately known or personally held, to authenticate that the user is really who he or she claims to be. This could be a plastic card, fingerprint, or recognizable voice pattern. However, by far the most common authentication means is for the user to enter a private password. From here on, we shall consider only passwords as authentication means. Other forms of token may become common in the future, but that will not change the validity of our position on passwords.

3. *Authorization.* The authenticated user is then permitted to perform only those actions, for instance, to access and update certain files, execute certain programs or transactions, and read certain documents, that have been preauthorized.

To examine the security effectiveness of logical access control mechanisms in preventing unauthorized access, we must again consider these three logical steps independently.

First, the user ID has a limited security role. If a personnel code such as employee number is chosen for the User ID, then such codes may be general knowledge within the organization. User IDs are often required to be entered in cleartext and can therefore be seen by passersby or obtained from printout. If doubling as an account code, they will appear on invoices for computer usage that may pass through many hands. User IDs that become known to employees who leave the business with the knowledge, as well as contract staff and visitors, effectively become public knowledge. Thus, although it serves to distinguish each individual who may use the computer, a User ID may have no security value at all; it represents (only) a "claim to be" a certain person.

The authenticating password is a different matter. If the password is properly constructed, and if the user keeps it secret and private, not easily guessable, and changes it periodically, then a password can provide a highly effective security mechanism. The crucial word, of course, is "if." It is a matter of common knowledge within large data processing installations, confirmed by published articles in computer journals and by newspaper stories of computer "break-ins," that user password discipline is often poor. Passwords are written down or are easily guessable strings or names associated with the user. Passwords are seldom changed, and then only because security or data processing management insists.

The third logical element, authorization processes, are usually well designed and enforceable. Timesharing systems, for example, will commonly allow an authenticated user to access only "public" program libraries or data or programs that he or she has personally entered or created. Extension of access rights to other users requires some positive action by the data owner or a security administrator. Likewise, properly designed transaction-processing systems can be made completely inaccessible to a given User ID unless that User ID has been specifically authorized to execute certain transactions by a security administrator. Authorization mechanisms have received the greatest attention by designers of security systems. For example, the U.S. Department of Defense "Trusted Computer Systems Evaluation Criteria" concentrates very heavily on authorization mechanisms. Generally speaking, therefore, at reasonably low administrative overhead cost, authorization rights to access data can be automatically enforced and do not interfere unduly with business data processing needs.

It is obvious from the foregoing that the weak link in the chain of logical access security is the password. Users of business data processing services are motivated much more by their desire to get on with their computing than by a concern for data security (generally, users have a low perception of risk consistent with management views); password discipline is not normally enforced, and hence password discipline is poor.

Attempting to enforce password discipline by exhortation or supervisory methods is ineffective. In today's business conditions the policing of a large population of users with terminals at home and elsewhere is not practicable. Such effort is in any case unpopular; it smacks of bureaucracy. Therefore, this analysis and train of reasoning lead to the idea of developing a specification that would require the computer itself to enforce logical access security, automatically as far as possible, at each stage of use from sign-on to sign-off. The specification should pay particular attention to enforcing password discipline.

AUTOMATED LOGICAL ACCESS CONTROL STANDARD

Description

ALACS has as its objective to specify an optimum set of logical access controls to provide adequate security for typical confidential business data; these controls are to be automatically enforced by the computer's operating system, and if necessary, supplemented by the application system. Where not automatically enforceable because of system limitations, ALACS should provide maximum computer assistance for the manual administration of security.

A full specification of ALACS is given at the end of this appendix, and the security objective for each requirement is explained. ALACS contains no new security features that have not at some time been proposed or implemented by some computer supplier. Many of the requirements for passwords are described in "Guidelines on User Authentication Techniques."[25] However, a survey of the logical access controls of twelve software systems from seven unique combinations of leading hardware and software suppliers showed that none met ALACS completely and most had several significant weaknesses.

The novelty of ALACS is only that it covers all aspects of logical access control requirements for typical business data in one statement and that it specifies a sign-on protocol that maximizes automatic enforcement of password discipline in a user-friendly way. The parts of ALACS concerned with access authorization mechanisms are already standard practice on many suppliers' computer systems.

Publishing ALACS as a proposed standard serves two goals:

1. In the short term, an organization can compare its existing computer logical access control mechanisms with ALACS to identify weaknesses in security effectiveness. These weaknesses can then be rectified by in-house software modifications or brought to the computer supplier's attention; alternatively, the risk of the weakness can be consciously accepted. At best, security is improved; at worst, awareness of security vulnerability is heightened.

2. In the longer term, ALACS should stimulate debate in the business data processing community and, especially, standardization bodies. The debate will no doubt produce suggestions to improve ALACS. With increased customer pressure and public concern arising from the computer trespassing threat, computer manufacturers and suppliers of security packages should find it worthwhile to implement ALACS fully.

A full and uniform implementation of ALACS would not only bring a great improvement in computer security over the current level, it would generally help make computers easier to use. Today each business computer system has its own unique sign-on procedures and security mechanism. Imagine the parallel if every time you rented a car it was necessary to get out a manual to work out how to start the engine and drive off. Car manufacturers have evolved a standard user-friendly person-machine interface, and increasingly that interface incorporates safety-enforcement mechanisms (such as reminders about seat-belt wearing), analogous to ALACS' requiring computers to enforce security. Although "standard" in a conceptual sense, however, each car's interface is realized in practice in a unique way as far as detailed presentation and aesthetics are concerned. Likewise, ALACS is a conceptual specification. Details of presentation are left to the implementor.

A standard such as ALACS, therefore, has wider implications than security. The improvements in computer-user acceptability and productivity that would follow wide-scale implementation of ALACS, especially for large organizations using computers from many suppliers, will, in the long term, be as valuable as its security benefit.

Use

Objective

To specify an optimum set of logical processes that can be implemented on a computer to control access to confidential data and text held on the computer to maintain adequate security.

Scope

Any computer whose use is shared by a closed community of users, any of whom may use the computer or access files through terminals, microcomputers, and so on for certain preauthorized purposes, or where the data or text that are held are either

- Confidential to the organization or part of the organization using the computer
- Subject to other need-to-know restrictions (e.g., for internal control reasons, personal privacy, etc.)

Terminology

In this standard the word *computer* is used to encompass any computer, system or subsystem, shared intelligent workstation, or group or network thereof with which a user communicates, in interactive or batch mode, and that is a separate entity from a security control viewpoint. The controls described within ALACS may be distributed over various processors within the "computer" as appropriate to its configuration and security needs.

Requirements

The following minimum requirements must be met. For each requirement the corresponding security objective is given alongside.

Requirement	Security Objective
A. *User ID.* A User ID, minimum six characters, must be assigned to each individual user, which is unique to that computer. The computer will not allow two or more terminals to be signed on simultaneously with the same User ID.	Inhibits sharing of User IDs and emphasizes individual accountability for usage and security.
Although assigned to an individual person, a User ID may belong to one or more recognized groups of User IDs that share common access authorizations. (See C.2.a below.)	Helps simplify administration of access authorizations.
B. *Passwords.* Each individual User ID must have an associated password, which the user is instructed to keep private, with the following characteristics:	Password is the key to authenticating that the user is indeed the individual identified by the User ID.
1. *Length.* Minimum of six alphanumeric or special characters, excluding blanks.	Makes password harder to guess by trial and error or to discover from systematic testing.
2. *Frequency of change.* The computer will force a password to be changed within D days of the last change, where D is an installation parameter with maximum ninety-nine days, default thirty days.	Forced password changing reduces the security exposure if an existing password has become known to persons other than the password owner. Forced changing also heightens general user security consciousness.

Requirement	Security Objective
3. *Repeatability*. The computer will maintain a list of the last P passwords used by the User ID and will not accept an attempt to change to a password already used and still in the list. P is an installation parameter with a minimum of ten passwords.	Inhibits the user's trying to beat the enforced password changing control.
4. *Initialization*. When a new User ID is established, it will be given an "expired" password (see C.1.c below)—that is, one that must be changed at the first attempted sign-on by the User ID.	Prevents the person allocating User IDs from knowing the password that will be used by the user concerned.
5. *Encryption*. All passwords will be stored in the computer in one-way encrypted form. A password entered during an interactive sign-on or a batch job submission will be immediately encrypted at the time of entry, and thereafter never displayed in cleartext.	Prevents a system programmer or someone working in "privileged" mode (see C.3 below) from obtaining passwords and thereby being able to impersonate any User ID.

C. *Logical access control*
  1. *Sign-on (identification-authentication) phase*
  Sign-on will follow the procedure below, from the point where the computer is ready to accept identification of the user by a User ID.	

a. Computer invites sign-on by requesting entry of the User ID in an indicated field. If accepted, the computer proceeds with step b. If not accepted, the computer allows up to two more attempted entries, and then if still unsuccessful:
  • logs all unsuccessfully tried User IDs;
  • alerts operator or system security administrator;
  • (if appropriate) disconnects the terminal.
	Procedure is designed to help the genuine user but inhibit someone trying to find an acceptable User ID by trial and error.

b. Computer invites entry of password, in an indicated field, but provides a "blot" (or inhibits display or printing) for that field so	Procedure is designed to help the genuine user but inhibit a casual observer from seeing the password or someone trying to guess a password by trial and error.

Requirement	Security Objective
that the entered password cannot be read. User enters password, and if successful, the computer proceeds with step c. If unsuccessful, the computer allows up to two more attempted entries, and if still unsuccessful: • logs all unsuccessfully tried passwords; • alerts operator or system security administrator; • (if appropriate) disconnects the terminal. Note: The computer should enforce a time delay of at least two seconds between repeated attempted entries of a password.	Inhibits someone successfully using a computer to generate passwords systematically to gain entry.
c. The computer checks if today the password is more than E days from the date of expiration (E is an installation parameter, usually set to 20 percent of the forced change period D). If the password is still more than E days from the expiration, the computer proceeds with step f.	To be as helpful as possible the computer gives advance warning to a user whose password is due to expire imminently.
d. If the password is within E days of expiration but is still unexpired, the computer issues a warning giving the number of days remaining before the password must be changed. Alternatively, if the password expires today or is already expired, the computer informs the user that the password must be changed immediately.	
e. The computer issues an invitation to change the password, indicating the format and supplying a "blot" (or inhibiting display or printing). The user may ignore the invitation to change by pressing Return unless the password is already expired or expires today. If the user enters a new password, the computer invites a repeat en-	The computer helps the user change password and enforces change of an expired password. A changed password is requested a second time to avoid problems that would be caused by a typing error during the first entry and to reinforce the new password in the user's memory.

Requirement	Security Objective
try to validate the first entry (similarly concealed) and continues until two successive identical passwords are entered.	
f. The computer issues a message stating the date and time when the last successful sign-on was made.	Provides a check for the user that his or her User ID has not been used without the user's knowledge.
Batch Job or message submission from an interactive terminal or workstation:	
g. The computer will allow a batch job or message to be submitted for execution or sent from an interactive terminal or workstation only if the batch job or message is associated with the same User ID/password combination used for initial sign-on.	Prevents a user from signing on under one User ID with associated authorizations and then creating and submitting a job with a different authorization.
h. Sign-on proceeds essentially as in interactive mode, except the computer does not provide guiding messages and if any step is unsuccessful, the job is canceled, with the appropriate explanation.	
2. *Processing (authorization) phase*	
a. Any computer to which the User ID may gain access will control, using information provided by the owner of the object concerned:	Each User ID should be limited in what use can be made of the computer by pre-agreed need-to-know considerations.
• The list of objects (programs, transactions, files, etc.) to which the User ID is allowed access either individually or by membership of a recognized group or of preregistered attributes.	
• The level of access (read, copy, update, create-delete, execute) allowed to the objects.	
Additionally, the computer will warn the user (interactive mode) or cancel the job (batch mode) if the user tries to access beyond the authorized range or levels.	
b. The list of User IDs, or recognized groups of User IDs, that	The rules and mechanisms for changing access authorizations must be clearly and

Requirement	Security Objective
may access any object and the associated level of access may be changed only by • the User ID that individually created the object, • the object's owner (if such is established), or • the system security administrator working in privileged access mode (see below).	coherently established; they will vary depending on the type of computing service. Timesharing and office systems usually allow only the creator of an object to change the access authorizations. In contrast, a community of users sharing a common database is better regulated by a system security administrator acting on behalf of the database owner.
c. Any major subsystem executing on the computer that is shared by users with different need-to-know requirements and is treated as a single object by the computer's security system must itself provide its own authorization scheme along the lines of 2.a above.	The computer's security system may not be able to cope with incompatible security conventions of a "foreign" subsystem. The latter must therefore provide its own authorization mechanisms.
d. If a terminal or workstation is inactive for more than T minutes, the associated User ID will be automatically signed off. T will be an installation parameter with a default of fifteen minutes.	Prevents someone from using a terminal that has been left by a user who forgot to sign-off.
As an alternative to sign-off, the computer blanks the terminal screen and requires reentry of the user's password to resume the session.	Alternative caters to the case where the overhead due to sign-on or sign-off is unacceptable.
3. *Privileged Access* A privileged access mode will be available to a system security administrator for maintenance of all security and logical access control parameters, but only for those purposes. Privileged access will not be needed for any application programming or use of an application or utility program.	A privileged access mode is essential for security administration, such as establishing and deleting User IDs, changing certain types of access authorizations, etc. Such a privileged access mode must itself be protected from unauthorized use to at least the ALACS standard.
4. *Logging* All unsuccessful sign-on attempts and all unsuccessful access attempts during processing (both of range and levels) will be recorded in a log in the computer concerned, available only in privileged access mode. All	A log of attempted security violations is an essential defense mechanism to help a system security administrator discover apparent deliberate attempted violations.

Requirement	*Security Objective*
log message types will be uniquely coded, and date and time stamped to enable analysis. Analysis programs will highlight suspicious repeatedly unsuccessful sign-on or access attempts.	
5. *Authorization Maintenance* Administrative procedures will be established for each computer such that:	Sound procedures to administer User IDs are an essential counterpart to the computer-enforceable security measures.
a. If an individual leaves the organization, any individual User ID is immediately canceled.	
b. If an individual's job is changed, then any consequential changes of the individual's authorization to access programs, transactions, data, etc., are immediately affected.	
D. *Optional Refinements*	
1. *Physical Terminal* constrained to certain User IDs. The computer may allow only certain User IDs to sign on to certain physical terminals.	This is a valuable option for situations where specific computer processing should be possible only from certain terminals that could be at a specific secure location, equipped with certain security features, etc., due to the need to handle particularly sensitive data.
2. *Dialup.* An indication of whether or not access via a dialup port is allowed will be associated with each User ID. An attempt to use dialup when not authorized will result in failure to sign on.	Anyone wanting to obtain a User ID–password combination by trial and error will probably need the privacy of a remote dialup link to make the attempt. Therefore, limiting dialup access to known users who have valid reasons for dialup can limit this security risk.
3. *Unused User IDs.* If a User ID is unused for more than, say, ninety days, the computer logs that fact so that the system security administrator can ascertain whether the User ID is still needed.	A valuable aid for the system security administrator in isolating potentially defunct User IDs.

APPENDIX 4

Electronic Information Security Requirements Survey*

Budget Number _____ Preparer _____
Manager's Name _____ Date _____
Organization Name _____ /Dept./Div. Name or Number

INSTRUCTIONS

1. Ensure that the information above is completed.
2. Review the remaining instructions and the questionnaire.
3. The manager is responsible for completing the first section for the entire business center. The last section may be delegated to subordinates.
4. A copy of the last section must be completed for each system/software application.
5. If a response of nonapplicable (N/A) is used, explain the reason why.
6. Please type or neatly print any narrative.
7. A copy of corporate policy is included.

Note: If you use no electronic information processing (computers, terminals, telecopiers, word processors, printers) in your function, return this package with just the top of this page filled in.

ORGANIZATION AND ADMINISTRATION SECURITY

		Yes	No	N/A
Policy	1. Do you and your people understand the security requirements specified in corporate policy?	___	___	___
New employee briefings	2. Are new employees performing digital information processing given thorough briefings on the policies, regulations, and practices of the organization with respect to information security?	___	___	___

*Source: Carl Grovanz, Xerox Corporation.

Yes No N/A

User responsibility	3. Are systems users aware of their primary responsibility for the security of their information?	___ ___ ___
Technical security understanding	4. Do data processing-systems-telecommunications people understand the information value factors?	___ ___ ___
Supervision of critical positions	5. Do you provide effective supervision of employees in critical positions and supervisory reaction to job performance problems that indicate potential security exposures?	___ ___ ___
Job rotation	6. Is it practice to rotate periodically those positions that have a potential for exposure?	___ ___ ___
Job backup	7. Do you have backup (personnel, hardware, procedures) to perform all electronic information systems functions?	___ ___ ___
Contingency planning	8. Is there a current plan to ensure operations during service interruptions or in case of disaster?	___ ___ ___
Employee termination policy	9. Are procedures in place to cause immediate restriction of a terminated or transferred employee's access to sensitive materials and areas including account numbers, passwords, and key cards?	___ ___ ___
Attempted violations	10. Do you have a procedure to record and report any attempted violation of local security functions?	___ ___ ___
Vendor/ contract services	11. Is value-factor information being processed in a vendor's computer, site, or with unique vendor software? If so,	
	a. Has a nondisclosure agreement been signed?	___ ___ ___
	b. Has a risk analysis been conducted?	___ ___ ___
	c. Are there regular reviews and reporting of the vendor's security?	___ ___ ___
Phase reviews	12. Is security addressed during each phase review (initiation, definition, analysis, design, development, implementation) of any major system development project?	___ ___ ___

Yes No N/A

Irregularly
changed
passwords

13. Are passwords changed irregularly, but at least quarterly, on termination or resignation of employees having had access to the combinations or on compromise?

—— —— ——

Computer
inventory
controls

14. Is there inventory control of computer equipment, hardware, replacement parts, unused media, and supplies at all locations from arrival to end of useful life?

—— —— ——

Removable
storage

15. Are there procedures and controls used in the management of removable machine-readable storage?

—— —— ——

Shared
accounts

16. Is the same computer account or access control used by more than one person?

—— —— ——

Key personnel
directory

17. Are names and telephone numbers of key personnel to be called in case of emergencies clearly posted in all critical areas?

—— —— ——

Security
subsystem
administration

18. Is there a formal assignment of security subsystem administration for systems processing classified data and all data base systems?

—— —— ——

Overall
security
administration

19. Is there a formal administration function for digital information?

—— —— ——

20. Is account usage and chargeback verified for each billing?

—— —— ——

21. Is an up-to-date list of all purchased and leased hardware and software maintained?

—— —— ——

Portable
computer/
terminal

22. Is the use of portable computers or terminals controlled by a sign-out log or assigned to an individual responsible for knowing its whereabouts?

—— —— ——

Conflicting
responsibilities

23. Does anyone using facilities, equipment, or supplies software have conflicting responsibilities that contribute to a security risk, for example, report generation, and report destruction and report control; programmer, and computer operator and operating system maintenance?

—— —— ——

Level 1: Physical Security

DIGITAL INFORMATION PROCESSING DEVICE INVENTORY

Please complete for your function:

COMPUTERS

MANUFACTURER					
MODEL					
QUANTITY					

WORD PROCESSORS				REMOTE JOB ENTRY	
Mfg./Model				Mfg./Model	
Quantity				Quantity	

TERMINALS/ CRTS		PRINTERS		TRANSCEIVERS	
Video	Hard Copy	*Low Speed	High Speed	Manual	Automatic

*Low speed is less than 120 characters per second

		Yes	No	N/A

The following questions relate to access controls:

		Yes	No	N/A
Access controls	24. Do you restrict and control access to computing facilities?	___	___	___
Monitoring personnel	25. Is monitoring conducted for nonoperational personnel who are permitted access?	___	___	___
Access codes	26. Are access codes changed regularly for digital access facilities?	___	___	___
Secondary access	27. Is there access to any controlled area from a secondary point such as service doors, windows, etc.?	___	___	___

Complete this section if value-factor data is processed:

Classified data	28. Is classified data processed? If no, go on to Question 37.	___	___	___

Yes No N/A

		Yes	No	N/A
Unauthorized access	29. Are devices that are used to access or process value-factor information located in an access controlled area?	___	___	___
Visitor control	30. Are visitors to individual areas processing value-factor data identified and logged on entrance and exit?	___	___	___
Proper identification/ authorization	31. Is positive identification and authorization required for entering controlled areas of a facility processing value-factor information?	___	___	___
Latent impressions	32. Do latent impressions remain to be picked up after processing? (e.g., typewriter ribbons.)	___	___	___
Sanitizing/ erasing machine-readable media	33. Are procedures for sanitizing or erasing classified media enforced?	___	___	___
Waste containers	34. Are containers readily available for disposal of classified waste materials?	___	___	___
Lockable storage	35. Is lockable storage used for value-factor data?	___	___	___
Secure area	36. Is high-value-factor data processed only on computers or terminals in secure areas?	___	___	___

The remaining questions on this page pertain only to computer operations under your control.

		Yes	No	N/A
Computer operations	37. Does your function operate a computer? If no, go on to Question 44.	___	___	___
Security feature availability	38. Do you provide, on request, a description of available security features for users, system designers, or programmers?	___	___	___
Variety of security features	39. Do you provide for all computers a variety of protective features that include suitable elements from each of the following categories:			
	a. Level 1—Physical Security?	___	___	___
	b. Level II—Organizational and procedural security?	___	___	___

Yes No N/A

    c. Level III—Hardware and software
       security elements? ___ ___ ___

    d. Level IV—Encryption? ___ ___ ___

Storage media devices 40. Do operators and users of devices creating information storage media apply a combination of protective measures that

    a. Positively protect and control all such media? ___ ___ ___

    b. Prevent the release of media containing information to any individual, unless specifically authorized? ___ ___ ___

    c. Ensure that any shipment or transfer of such media between locations is by courier, insured express, sealed mail, or equivalent? ___ ___ ___

    d. When media containing value-factor information is moved between locations, is the value factor clearly marked on the media container or reel? ___ ___ ___

    e. Are formal records maintained of the status, location, and disposition of each such medium? ___ ___ ___

Data center supervision 41. Do you provide active supervision of all activities, including positive management control over and prior approval of

    a. All operating system maintenance actions? ___ ___ ___

    b. All hardware maintenance actions? ___ ___ ___

    c. All initial processor loading? ___ ___ ___

    d. All settings of system clocks? ___ ___ ___

    e. All changes to operating documentation (e.g., runbooks, job tickets, processing instructions)? ___ ___ ___

Disaster avoidance 42. Are facilities, both central and remote, constructed to provide the minimum level of protection as specified in policy against natural disasters and against persons intent on destroying property? ___ ___ ___

Yes No N/A

System/   43. Is a system log, console log, etc.,
console logs   sequentially numbered or otherwise
                      controlled to ensure a complete and
                      auditable review of all actions?   ___ ___ ___

44. If you have any further questions or comments on the first two sections
    (Level II and Level I), please provide them below:

    _____

    _____

    _____

    _____

    _____

                                          Labor
                                          Hours   Expense Capital

45. Provide an estimate of the number of hours
    and additional expenses and capital required
    for your budget center to comply with the
    organizational and physical aspects of this
    questionnaire.   _____   _____   _____

DATA SECURITY
(BY SYSTEM/SOFTWARE APPLICATION)

Application Name _____ Preparer's Name _____
Acronym _____ Telephone Ext. _____
Description _____

_____

_____

_____

_____

_____

APPLICATION TYPE CODE	PROCESSING TYPE	DATA CENTER LOCATION _____
☐ Finance	☐ Batch	D.P. equipment
☐ Research	☐ On-line	Used _____
☐ Design	☐ Real-time	MFG. _____
☐ Simulation		Model _____
☐ Data acquisition		
☐ Control		
☐ Other _____		
_____		

Main Language		Subsidiary Language		Number of Programs		Lines of Code	

Year System Was Installed		Economic End-of-Life Forecast		Planned Replacement Year		Estimated Replacement Costs $000	

		Yes	No	N/A
Value factor: User assigned	1. Has the user assigned a value factor to all input documents, displays, reports, and procedures?	___	___	___
Information security assigned classifications	2. Have the individuals involved with electronic information systems reflected the above value factor in the files, programs, and documentation?	___	___	___
Input and output volume count comparison	3. Are there procedures and software to ensure that users compare input-output volume against predicted requirements?	___	___	___
Input and output data movement controls	4. Are there transmittal documents to effect positive controls (such as traceability) over data being moved between user areas and the computer center?	___	___	___
Password protection capability	5. Does the computer contain a password capability? If no, go on to Question 10.	___	___	___
Password protection system	6. Is a comprehensive password protection system provided to include initiation, disbursement, storage, and change of password?	___	___	___
Password generation	7. Are there procedures and software to ensure generation of passwords that are difficult to guess or determine programatically?	___	___	___
Password print suppress	8. Are passwords inhibited from display when entered through a terminal?	___	___	___

Yes No N/A

		Yes	No	N/A
Password classification	9. Are passwords classified and protected the same as the highest value-factor information shielded by that password?	___	___	___
Program change control log	10. Are there procedures or software or both to effect complete control over program changes, such as change logs?	___	___	___
Application system test	11. Are specific procedures, software, and guidelines used to ensure thorough testing of application systems before operational status is acquired?	___	___	___
System standards	12. Are there procedures and software to ensure that all systems use departmentally accepted or published standards?	___	___	___
Data isolation controls	13. Are there procedures, software, and hardware to isolate test programs from production programs and test data from live data?	___	___	___
Data integrity	14. Do effective control features ensure data integrity (e.g., batch totals, control totals)?	___	___	___
System security features	15. Are the system security features described fully in documentation and acceptable to the users for everyday practical application?	___	___	___
	16. Are there instructions for control of passwords, authorizations, and other security functions?	___	___	___
Access denied delay	17. Does the security system cause a delay to be introduced whenever an access attempt is denied?	___	___	___
Programming changes	18. Is there a management approval in place for authorization of all program changes?	___	___	___
System documentation	19. Is the system fully documented?	___	___	___
	20. Is the documentation stored in a secure environment (not in an individual's desk)?	___	___	___
Documentation controls	21. Are there procedures, software, and special facilities to control access to the system and application documentation?	___	___	___

Yes No N/A

Improper log-on controls	22. Are there procedures and software to detect repeated attempts to log-on?	___ ___ ___
Processing time controls	23. Is there a check of actual time of use against expected time for the application?	___ ___ ___
Tape/disk/ card movement controls	24. Is there ensured control of removable media movement through the operations area? This includes a capability for traceability and accountability, basically a requirement for external labels on all media?	___ ___ ___
Modular design of systems	25. Is simple modular system design and structured programming used?	___ ___ ___

THE REMAINING QUESTIONS PERTAIN ONLY TO SYSTEMS PROCESSING OR CREATING VALUE-FACTOR (VF) DATA

VF data	26. Do you process VF data? If no, go on to Question 44.	___ ___ ___
Forms control	27. Is forms control used for VF reports at remote sites to require operator intervention before reports can be printed?	___ ___ ___
Handling classified data	28. Do systems that process or create VF information include procedures that issue proper identification, marking, and handling of classified information?	___ ___ ___
	29. Is the output securely wrapped?	___ ___ ___
Casual observation protection	30. Are VF inputs and outputs protected from casual observation at all times?	___ ___ ___
Media storage classifications	31. Are color-coded labels affixed to all VF storage media moved between locations?	___ ___ ___
Input and output segregation	32. Are VF input and output kept separate from non-VF data?	___ ___ ___
Input and output data storage	33. Do you provide lockable storage for VF data, programs, and reports?	___ ___ ___

Yes No N/A

		Yes	No	N/A
Sensitive file access log	34. Do you log all accesses by system programs or application programs to files designated as VF?	___	___	___
Classified report marking	35. Is each page of a VF batch report sequentially numbered?	___	___	___
	36. Is the last page so noted?	___	___	___
	37. Is each page, and front and back covers, stamped with VF symbol or marked through program-generated printing in the upper right-hand corner?	___	___	___
Use of vendors	38. Is VF information processed in a vendor's computer, site, or with unique vendor software?	___	___	___
Storage purge	39. Is an overwrite or erase of all types of storage accomplished after use for VF processing?	___	___	___
HI-VF data	40. Do you process HI-VF data? If no, go on to Question 44.	___	___	___
Remote encryption capability	41. Do you provide encryption capability for storing and transmitting HI-VF data at remote data processing facilities?	___	___	___
Encryption for transport	42. Are HI-VF data to be transported by a third party outside the computer facility encrypted?	___	___	___
Communication encryption	43. Is encryption provided for HI-VF data passing over communication lines?	___	___	___

44. If you have any further questions or comments, please provide them below:

_____

_____

_____

_____

_____

	Labor Hours	Expense	Capital
45. Provide an estimate of the number of hours and additional expenses/capital required to update this application to achieve compliance per the questionnaire.	___	___	___

Data sensitivity 46. Does the system contain any of the following or similar types of data? *Check those included.*

Long-range and contingency plans	_____	Product life plans and reports	_____
Major new ventures	_____	Program papers	_____
Acquisition or sale of business or properties	_____	Early and sensitive product/system specifications	_____
Major curtailment of operations or personnel reductions	_____	Competitive assessments and comparisons	_____
Business strategy or product technology letters and reports	_____	Strategic alternatives	_____
Position papers	_____	Major personnel or facility changes	_____
Future product design and developments	_____	Consolidated plans	_____
		Other (explain)	_____

APPENDIX 5

Checklist for Security Review

CORPORATE ELECTRONIC SECURITY REVIEW

FOR _____ Review of _____
BY _____ Date _____
WITH _____ Title _____
SECURITY MANAGER _____
INFORMATION SECURITY COORDINATOR _____

I. General
    1. Are current electronic security standards available for reference?
    2. Are security coordinators appointed, are they supported by management, and are they fulfilling a positive role?
    3. Are *Information Handling Regulations* booklets available for reference? Are the regulations understood and followed?
    4. Is there an active security program?
        • Are security posters and a general awareness of security evident?
        • Are security booklets available at this location?
        • Does the security manager have the security handbook?
    5. Is physical security up to company standards (with proper emergency procedures, physical access controls, visitors escorted, etc.)?
    6. Are periodic security review reports provided to management?
    7. Are appropriate confidentiality or disclosure agreements signed?
    8. Show organization chart.
II. Data Center, Telecommunications
    1. Is general center and operations security sufficient for processing of corporate *private data* under routine operating conditions?
    2. Are special controlled areas established as appropriate (e.g., operations, media library)?
    3. Does the data center provide security services appropriate to the needs of users (e.g., software packages, delivery services)?
    4. Are positive management controls established over the operating environment (e.g., changes to program libraries, changes to programs or documentation, quality control testing, setting of system clocks, maintenance of operations logs)?

5. Are output handling procedures in line with the requirements of *Information Handling Regulations?*
6. Are printers properly controlled or are classified outputs properly controlled?
7. Are logical access control packages properly administered and are changes to users' access authorizations status promptly effected by a formal process?
8. Are contingency plans prepared as appropriate?
9. If *company registered* information is processed, are proper controls applied, including encryption?
10. Is security responsibility clearly assigned and are sufficient resources available?
11. Are employees periodically reminded of security responsibilities?
12. Are work areas clean and orderly?
13. Are effective emergency systems in place?

III. Office, Personal, and Distributed Computing
1. Are individual users aware of personal information security responsibilities (does each employee have *Information Handling Regulations* and *Guide for People Using Electronic Equipment in the Office, Security Guide,* and know-how to protect electronic information in his or her control)?
2. Are individual workplaces maintained in a clean, orderly, and secure condition (company clean desk policy)?
3. Are workstations or terminals shut down or placed in a quiet state when the user is absent for more than two hours or as appropriate?
4. Are documents and media properly stored and protected?
5. Are backup media files created and stored in a safe place?
6. Are logical access management controls in use?
7. Are office and section security coordinators appointed and active?
8. Do Internet system administrators monitor and encourage security among network users?
9. Is password discipline observed?
10. Are contingency plans prepared as appropriate?
11. If *company registered* information is processed, are proper protection elements applied?

IIIa. Corporate Internet Operations
1. Are managers responsible for network operations and system administrator aware of general security requirements?
2. Is the *Internet Security Guide* available?
3. Are privileges controlled through written authorizations for a minimum number of people?
4. Is password discipline (including password construction, distribution, secure maintenance, and changes) observed per standards?
5. Is a procedure in place to manage special situations requiring temporary authorizations (e.g., vacations, holidays)?

6. Are privileges restricted to systems analysts only (no maintenance technicians, managers, etc.)?
7. Is there an established backup cycle, formalized in procedure?
8. Do users understand security requirements per *Information Handling Regulations?*

IV. Applications Systems Design and Implementation
1. Do project management phases include security considerations?
2. Is prime user involved in security-related design decisions during system development?
3. Is security a consideration in individual employee application development?
4. Are documentation packages afforded proper security?
5. Are change control procedures formally specified?
6. Do systems designers and programmers have their own copies of *Company Electronic Security Standards* and *Information Handling Regulations?*
7. Are access authorization processes specified in system procedures?

V. Outside Services and Connections
1. Are there management approvals or controls over outside connections or services?
2. Are *company classified* data processed by non-company services? If so, is an exception approval on file and are suitable protection steps taken?
3. Are external connections available through other than Internet mail gateways?
4. Have all contractors and their employees signed disclosure agreements?
5. Where dialup connections are in use, are accesses controlled by use of security software, port control systems, or other appropriate means?
6. Are suitable administrative records and procedures in place to identify and control access authorizations?
7. Are applicable privacy laws observed?
8. Are export and import regulations followed?

Recommended Periodicals and Professional Groups

RECOMMENDED PERIODICALS

Datapro Reports on Information Security, Datapro Research Corporation, Delran, N.J., 08075.

Computers and Security, Elsevier Science Publishing Company, 52 Vanderbilt Avenue, New York, N.Y., 10017.

RECOMMENDED PROFESSIONAL GROUPS FOR INFORMATION SECURITY

American Society for Industrial Security (ASIS), Committees on Proprietary Information and Computer Security, 1655 North Ft. Meyer Drive, Suite 1200, Arlington, Va. 22209.

Association for Computing Machinery, Special Interest Group, Security, Audit, and Control (SIGSAC), ACM, 11 West 42nd Street, New York, N.Y. 10036.

Computer Society of the Institute of Electrical and Electronic Engineers (IEEE), Technical Committee on Security and Privacy, 1730 Massachusetts Avenue, N.W., Washington, D.C. 20036.

Information Systems Security Association (ISSA), P.O. Box 10246, Newport Beach, Calif. 92658.

References

1. *The New York Times,* Sept. 16, 1987, p. D17.
2. Schweitzer, James A. *Protecting Information on Local Area Networks* (Stoneham, MA: Butterworth Publishers, 1988), p. 23.
3. Diebold, John. "IRM—New directions in management," *Infosystems,* Oct. 1979, p. 41.
4. Eells, Richard, and Peter Nehemkis. *Corporate Intelligence and Espionage* (New York: Macmillan, 1984), p. 75.
5. Synnott, William R., and William H. Gruber. *Information Resource Management* (New York: John Wiley & Sons, 1981), p. 128.
6. Meyer, N. Dean, and Mary E. Boone. *The Information Edge* (New York: McGraw-Hill, 1987), p. 41.
7. Bottom, Norman R., Jr., and Robert R.J. Gallati. *Industrial Espionage—Intelligence Techniques and Countermeasures* (Stoneham, MA: Butterworth Publishers, 1984), p. 5.
8. Pooley, James. *The Executive's Guide to Protecting Proprietary Business Information and Trade Secrets* (Chicago: Probus Publishing Co., 1987), p. 49.
9. Halbrecht, Herbert L. (quote from) "Business needs a new breed of EDP managers," by Richard L. Nolan. *Harvard Business Review,* March-April 1976, p. 133.
10. Toffler, Alvin. Interview, *Software,* Jan. 1981, p. 24.
11. Martin, James. *Strategy for Distributed Data Processing.* (Englewood Cliffs, NJ: Prentice Hall, 1981), p. 376.
12. Martin, p. 379.
13. Strassman, Paul A. *Information Payoff* (New York: Free Press, 1982), p. 243.
14. Pooley, p. 37
15. Marx, Peter (quote). "Liability in the information age," *Infoworld,* Aug. 16, 1986, p. 37.
16. Bottom and Gallati, p. 231.
17. "Dataview" (box), *Computerworld,* Aug. 24, 1987, p. 35.
18. Dingman, Cathy. "Good-bye, paperless dreams," *Computer and Communications Decisions,* Sept. 1987, p. 67.
19. Drucker, Peter F. *Innovation and Entrepreneurship* (New York: Harper & Row, 1985), p. 38.
20. Hoffman, Lance. *Modern Methods for Computer Security and Privacy* (Englewood Cliffs, NJ: Prentice Hall, 1977), p. 11.

21. Tuchman, W.L., and C.H. Meyer. *Efficacy of the Data Encryption Standard in Data Processing* (New York: IBM Corp., 1978).
22. Kent, Stephen T. "Protocol design considerations for network security," MIT Laboratory for Computer Science, NATO Advanced Studies Institute, Cambridge, MA, September 1978.
23. Rivest R., A. Shamir, and L. Adelman. *A Method for Obtaining Digital Signatures and Public Key Cryptosystems* (Cambridge, MA: MIT Press, 1977), LCS/TM82.
24. Parker, Donn B., Susan Nycum, and Ora S. Stephen. *Computer Abuse* (Menlo Park, CA: SRI International, 1973).
25. "Guidelines on User Authentication Techniques for Computer Network Access Control." Washington, DC, U.S. Federal Information Processing Standard Publication (FIPS PUB 83), Sept. 29, 1980.

Index